Developing
Resourceful Managers

John Morris
Professor of Management Development
Manchester Business School

John Burgoyne
Research Fellow
Manchester Business School

INSTITUTE OF PERSONNEL
MANAGEMENT

Central House, Upper Woburn Place

London WC1H 0HX

First published 1973

Reprinted 1976

00666261

Printed in Great Britain by
Lonsdale Universal Printing Ltd.

ISBN 0 85292 078 4

Contents

INTRODUCTION

Management development is often seen as an important but rather predictable activity: the skilled task of making sure that the enterprise is effectively managed, both in the present and the foreseeable future. The emphasis on predictability and control, especially in large organizations, has had the unintended effect of turning management development into the 'processing' of yet another organizational resource, albeit a singularly vital one. 'Developing managers' then becomes an affair for personnel specialists—a set of elaborate and sophisticated techniques rather than an exchange of valued ideas and the expression of strong feeling.

We are aware of the need for planning and control but also want to bring out the need for able managers to develop themselves. There is an inevitable contrast, and tension, between the organizational tendency to turn managers into conventional resources and the human tendency, not always successful, to manage one's self.

In their brief compass, these notes do not attempt to be systematic. They follow the somewhat meandering line of their authors' interests and personal experience. Chapter 1 is concerned with the homely metaphors used by experienced managers in talking about management and management development. Without leaning too heavily on these metaphors, we have found that they can be grouped into quite a revealing order.

In chapter 2, some brief case studies indicate the wide range of approaches to management development. In chapter 3, a simple 'model' is presented and discussed. Organizational life is seen as a flow of dramas, rituals and routines, and managers cannot avoid the responsibility for steering their way as best they can through the dramas, often of their own making. Dramas are divided into development dramas, which bring the organization to a new phase of development, and breakdown dramas, which are a disruption of normal activity.

In chapter 4, development dramas are linked with a set of functions: research and development, marketing, development finance, organization development and others. These are collectively termed 'development management'. Special attention is given to the use of projects in development management. Finally, chapter 5 considers selected aspects of management development in the future: the role of business schools and other development centres; the need for a new kind of management teacher; and the role of the personnel function in developing managers. We have linked this last aspect with 'organization development'.

However inconsistent these notes may be in other ways, they are consistently concerned with ideas, rather than with procedures or techniques. Our limited space has been given to expounding ideas that we have found helpful in discussing management issues with experienced managers. We leave to another occasion the relationship of these ideas to others current in the field, particularly those linked with personal development and organizational development. The book list in the appendix gives some indication of our intellectual debts. The responsibility for the views expressed is clearly our own.

1 Management thinking about management development

Professional personnel managers go into the 'fine texture' of course design, training methods and the evaluation of the outcomes of management training and development. When they think about the whole process of developing managers, some of them understandably look for systematic concepts and theories on which to hang their detailed practice. Other managers, in contrast, avoid thinking about the process as a whole because their experience has led them to believe that individuals and situations are so diverse that any kind of theorizing will do more harm than good, and is probably a sign of inexperience or over-optimism. As a result the professional in the field of management development tends to focus either on sophisticated theory or on detailed procedures.

Practising managers, on the other hand, who know about management development in the immediate context of their wide-ranging management responsibilities, often find quite homely, metaphorical ways of thinking about the process. For example, one senior manager in the Post Office told us that he wanted to 'grow his own timber'. Others have spoken of 'building' a good team or 'providing the seedcorn'. We have noted six metaphors that are particularly often used in the context of management development. They reveal a tendency that is obvious enough but is of great importance to our later discussion of approaches to management development. *People's thinking about management development usually matches their thinking about the process of management.* The senior man who wants to 'grow' managers sees them as doing rather different things from the manager who wants to 'build' them.

We shall consider each of the six metaphors in turn, giving brief examples of the way in which each of them is used and some of its implications. We then hope to show that the insights provided by these metaphors can be combined into a rather more formal model of management activities, from which some further thinking about management development can be derived.

1 The building metaphor

Building is an ancient craft and those using the building metaphor are duly aware of the gravity of the aspect of human affairs with which they are professionally concerned. They attach great importance to laying solid foundations, shaping the behaviour of the manager and keying it in to the established activities of the organization. When managers use this metaphor, they clearly have in mind the need to build a durable system of human relationships that will withstand competition and individual variability (in fact, will be 'as safe as houses').

This metaphor appeals to the feeling of practising managers for the concrete and tangible aspects of managerial work. Senior managers, on the production side in particular, like the idea of leaving a monument to their endeavours in the shape of an enduring human association—an establishment, one might say. The weakness of the metaphor follows from its strength. It conveys no sense of movement. It deals with change by resisting it. If we shift from thinking of Norman castles or Tudor manor houses to television masts able to stand up to high winds by giving to them, we are beginning to move from the building metaphor to the engineering metaphor.

2 The engineering metaphor

The managers using this metaphor find themselves

talking about modular components, stresses, friction, problems at the 'inter-face' between the moving parts of the system and the questions of 'design'. The ubiquitous theme of 'efficiency' is often related to the engineering metaphor. Management thinking about management training often shows clear signs of the influence of the metaphor: materials can be 'plugged in' or 'slotted in', training needs can be 'specified', and the programme can be 'designed' and 'engineered' to meet these requirements. Not surprisingly, the people taking part in such programmes are often described as 'products' of training. If they do not measure up to required standards of quality, they are in danger of becoming 'wastage'. Since the participants cannot be trusted to know whether they have learned something or not, they must be 'evaluated' by standardized measures of 'training effectiveness'. The use of programmed instruction is obviously a godsend to devotees of this metaphor.

The engineering metaphor, in its fullest development, totally ignores the problems of unanticipated circumstances and can only take into account those individual differences that fit into pre-established programmes. Recognition of these limitations opens the way for thinking about people in organic rather than mechanistic terms. The most elementary way of thinking about organic aspects of people is to see them as plants.

3 The agricultural metaphor

'In order to get good results, you have to sow the right seed and provide the right conditions, and then nature will do the rest'. This seems to be the essential theme of the agricultural metaphor. This way of thinking seems more common among older managers than among the young 'technocrats', who are more likely to take a rational, manipulative view of people as 'human resources' to be fitted in with the other resources which the firm has purchased in order to produce a profitable flow of goods and services. The agricultural metaphor is unusually elastic, even for a metaphor. We have noted three varieties in particular: the garden, the wood and the forest. These differ mainly in the amount of human control over the outcome, starting with the single plot of ground surrounding a house and ending with a way of life in its own right where development follows its own laws, which have little to do with people.

The gardener decides what kind of plants he wants, then chooses the right seeds, and uses his knowledge of the best conditions of growth to have the plants flowering at the time and place that he chooses. A well-planned garden will have plants flowering and bearing fruit at all seasons. Differing types of plants will be cleverly blended to fit together. Although the gardener may seem almost godlike to the uninitiated, he recognizes that nature is the real cause of the effects that he appears to be bringing about. His strength is in his knowledge of the characteristics of diverse species, and the conditions that they need for effective growth. In order to achieve the desired outcome, he has to fit in with the facts of life and these are likely to prove somewhat less tractable than the inorganic materials in the workshop.

Nevertheless, gardens are more orderly places than woods. A wood can look after itself but an untended garden quickly runs to waste. The order in a garden is that imposed (or at least, decided) by man. The order in a wood is natural. But the hand of man can still play an important part in maintaining and increasing the wood's good health. If people take an interest in a wood, they can unobtrusively remove dead wood and cut down some of the proliferation of young plants. The woodsman tries to strike a happy balance between his own planning efforts and those of the wood itself, viewed as a complex natural system.

When we shift from thinking about woods to forests, the growth in scale is almost alarming. The forest provides us with a powerful, even sinister, image of unchecked proliferation. It is at the furthest removed from the controlled order of a garden. Management development, it would seem, has little to do with the agricultural metaphor in this form. And yet the headlong career by which many highly successful managers have shot up their organizations, apparently without aid from trainers or developers, suggests something exotic, quite out of keeping with gardens or woods. Perhaps such people have been using the slow growing trees of taller growth as poles up which to climb, like some strange tropical vine or fungus. The image is startling and is given further possibilities by the next metaphor—zoological metaphor, which also comes in three forms.

4 The zoological metaphor

The variants of the zoological metaphor most often used are of the petshop, the zoo and the jungle. Unlike the agricultural metaphor, the zoological metaphor is concerned with creatures with a will of their own, possibly friendly, possibly dangerous. The weakest variant of the metaphor sees the manager as docile and tractable if he is treated well. We hear of the new man being 'broken in'. The qualities of loyalty, even devotion, and affection can only be evoked in the petshop approach by providing firm guidance and leadership.

Things get a little wilder when we move to the zoo— which is a planned environment for displaying animals to human advantage. Within the protective environment of the zoo, some animals get along well and for all we know prefer it to their 'natural environment'. However well fed and housed, other pine away and die. Even animals which look physically well may find themselves unable to procreate. As our understanding of animals deepens, so we devise new kinds of zoo which move even closer to the environment normally experienced by the animal, and the zoo becomes a 'sanctuary' or a 'reserve'. We then move imperceptibly to the third form of the metaphor, the image of nature untouched by man—the jungle.

In the jungle, many things happen that would appal the benevolent person. Infants are eaten or die of malnutrition. Fights occur. The apparent waste of resources is enormous. But underneath the apparent confusion, a complex balance is often established. The well meaning conservator or developer may find that, by upsetting the balance, he does more harm than good.

Clearly, the relationship between the rapidly proliferating plant in the forest and the wide-ranging predator in the jungle is very close. Both tell us something of the problems of formal, planned 'management development' in dealing with the strong, aggressive personalities who seem to flourish when left to themselves in a messy, unplanned environment. Such people often deride the lengthy programme of formal management training as 'Mickey Mouse' (petshop or zoo?). With such problems of the kinds of guidance that are appropriate to management development, we come to the next metaphor, which leaves the world of buildings, machines, plants and animals and comes directly to people. But not yet to people in their full health and strength (that must wait for a later metaphor) but people who have problems.

5 The medical metaphor

In many modern companies, especially those which are exploring the contributions that can be made by the behavioural sciences, one hears a good deal of discussion about the diagnosis and treatment of managerial problems. The medical terminology ramifies—into 'pathologies', 'symptoms', 'prognosis' all requiring an appropriate 'regimen'. Some managers would argue that these are not metaphors but accurate descriptions of reality. This claim illustrates a point of some importance: that metaphors can become a reality of their own. They are, after all, simple models of observation and experience and can therefore be expected to influence the manager's decisions and actions. But in our own experience, medical metaphors often run well ahead of the practice of the managers using them. The realities of 'managerial medicine' can be readily translated into much more homely terms. In a word, this metaphor encourages a certain pretentiousness.

An obvious weakness of the medical metaphor is that it focusses on sickness and disorder rather than health and normal functioning. Those who use this metaphor look at the organization through dark-tinted glasses; they are quick to detect problems rather than opportunities and breakdowns rather than radical improvements.

On the other hand, the great strength of this metaphor is its concern with re-establishing healthy functioning. It is also the first metaphor that we have discussed to centre on the experience of people rather than things, plants or animals. It is understandable that the medical metaphor should be applied to management development. The manager is often rightly seen as being surrounded by obstacles or as hampered by his own rigid attitudes. In the first place, he must find ways of removing the obstacles and in the second he must be helped to overcome his own personal 'hang-ups'. There have been other aspects of the medical metaphor for those who have been concerned with management development. The profession of the medical man has traditionally been highly prestigious. That of a training officer has been distinctly less so. If a choice has to be made between being a management trainer and a management doctor, there is no doubt which most people choose. There is also, without a doubt, a good deal of truth in the suggestion that organizational difficulties have a close resemblance to some forms of stress and breakdown on the individual level. All of this goes to justify the metaphor. It is clear, however, that managers who are unable to get beyond the medical metaphor have great difficulty in recognizing what managers do when they are working well rather than badly. This leads us to the last of our six metaphors, which grows out of military activities.

6 The military metaphor

In much of managers' thinking about management, war has dominated the scene. Management development then becomes rather like military training. Most of the language of business policy has been borrowed from the armed services. We talk of mobilizing a task force, getting the organization into action and managing by objectives. Business policy, borrowing from American practice, is often called 'corporate strategy'. Discussion of 'tactics' and 'logistics' follows hard on its heels. Rather more grimly, we think of the 'casualties' that must be endured in a successful strategy: the people who must be dispensed with, the companies that we must overwhelm and invade. In a hotly fought action or in the lull between actions, managers reflect on 'morale' and wonder whether they have enough 'dynamic leaders'.

None of this is surprising. Industrial and commercial activity in a capitalist society is highly competitive. Individual enterprises stake their capital along with that of others in a risk-taking activity, in which the production of socially necessary goods and services is almost a by-product of profitability. As in the armed services during a long campaign, the harshness and brutality are tempered by self-sacrifice and the warmth of comradeship. What begins as a crusade, if the war is long enough, can end up as a way of life.

Because of the enormous risks inherent in war, the armed services have traditionally put a great deal of emphasis on training. Such training is by no means limited to relevant knowledge and technical skills; it is concerned with forming appropriate attitudes and values: tenacity, self-discipline, courage, determination, loyalty, fortitude. Many of these qualities are esteemed by senior managers every bit as much as they are valued by the armed services. The metaphor grows close to the reality, and the comparison that has been drawn between some of the more demanding management training courses and commando battle training is by no means trivial.

It is from the armed services that we get the basic distinction between 'line' and 'staff' management: the first taking responsibility for the command of troops, in a hierarchical system of direct authority, and the second providing information, advice and interpretation of established policy.

This distinction becomes controversial in those aspects of the organization in which information, decision, action and learning from experience flow into one another rapidly, because a firm structure has not yet been established. This applies particularly to situations of high drama. In special service units, particularly designed for such situations (for example, commandos, parachutists, submariners) the whole unit is required to have combat competence, even though some parts of it may have 'staff' functions most of the time (for example, administration, intelligence, signals, transport).

Two other valuable distinctions come from the military metaphors: between the 'light' troops who open up positions with skill and daring, but lack the resources to consolidate, and the 'heavy' units which consolidate the gains and run the established system. If these are not controlled by a higher-level authority (general staff in command) the two disparate activities can get out of balance. On the one hand, opportunities will not be taken and insensitivity to the realities of a changing situation can set in; on the other, lines of communication can be over-extended and the whole enterprise become vulnerable to breakdown and defeat.

Training, therefore, becomes a vital and complex activity: training for general and functional control, for exploitation and consolidation for decision and for advisory services. One begins to wonder whether the military metaphor is merely metaphorical or is beginning to touch on life itself, though admittedly life that is very close to death, life in constant touch with emergency, maybe a 'world within a world' but in a sense a world of nightmarish implications.

The metaphors and reality

So we end our list of metaphors of management and the process of management development with a metaphor that presses a vital nerve rather than merely casually touching on one aspect of management activity. As the metaphors move from the non-human to the human, from the static to the dynamic, from the impoverished (metaphorically speaking) to the rich and complex, the gap between the metaphor and the reality narrows until one hardly knows which is metaphor and which is reality. Consider, for example, the sales manager briefing his sales representatives before a big sales campaign, telling of the penetration into the market, the gains that are expected, the sacrifices that will have to be made, the high costs in resources, the logistic details—is this not the reality of his work?

Perhaps the complex aspect of reality that the metaphors have caught very inadequately is the important part that love, trust and affection play in managerial life. In recent years, particularly in the larger firms, there has been a growing recognition of the importance of these motives and an attempt to foster them in management education and development programmes. A glance at the writings on 'human relations group training', 'sensitivity training', and 'T-groups' (T for training) reveals the importance of self and others, needs for growth, richness of experience and the like. It is odd that all of these are associated with something as traditionally hard-nosed as 'training', rather than with the broader concepts of development and education.

Two themes in management and management development

Our treatment of the six metaphors has been sketchy and in one or two places rather dismissive (for example, the more domesticated aspects of the agricultural and zoological metaphors have been given short shrift, although they may be of great practical value in fitting people to the more orderly kinds of managerial work). It may be useful at this point to look at the strengths of each of the metaphors. The building metaphor is useful in bringing out the structural aspects of organization and the stability and consistency of many kinds of management work. Together with the engineering metaphor, it reminds us of the impersonality and objectivity of many of the tasks managers are called upon to do. Many of the objectives and resources of organizations are not directly concerned with people as such, but with flows of money, materials and information. There is nothing sinister in metaphors which draw attention to this.

The agricultural metaphor draws attention to the contrast between rational intentions and natural processes and contingencies. Even the gardener must learn to respect nature in his small patch of growing things. Plants are not only different because of their environment but because of the genera to which they belong. The outcome of growth is a complex and in some respects unique outcome of the interaction of nature and nurture. The same point is made in the zoological metaphor but it brings out the vital factor of movement, the search for independence and the use of initiative. The medical metaphor draws attention to the hang-ups that prevent further growth of skill and sensitivity, and to the extraordinary complexity of the human personality and its vulnerability to breakdown. But, on the positive side, it also reminds us of the drive towards health and growth. Like the gardener, the best doctor does what he can, leaves the rest to nature and concerns himself with preventive measures.

Finally, the military metaphor focusses on aggresiveness and energy, on individual valour and determination, on the banding of great numbers of people into armies, disciplined to withstand deprivation, to strive for victory.

These metaphors can no doubt be grouped in many ways. But two themes seem particularly relevant. They are activity and passivity: the contrast between managers as *stable resources* and as *resourceful people*. Looked at from this point of view, the building and engineering metaphors enable us to see people as parts of a well-designed, purposeful structure, able to meet the requirements of their organizational specification. The medical and military metaphors, at the other end of the scale, bring out the initiative and energy of managers. The middle pair of metaphors are split between the two themes. The image of the garden or the petshop brings out the tractability of the manager; that of the forest or the jungle the independence and even wildness of managers as individuals, with wills of their own.

2 Some examples of management development

Before we go on to embody these themes in a model, we present three examples of large scale management development activities within organizations and institutions. Our aim is to illustrate that the differences in ways of thinking about management development correspond to, and are related to, differences in organizational and institutional approach to management development.

A public utility

Our first example of a management development programme is taken from a public utility, a type of organization that differs in many ways from most privately owned commercial organizations. A major difference is the nature of its product range. A private firm is free to try to sell a whole range of products and to develop new ones but the public utility is restricted to a single product, together with related appliances. Its managers believe that the 'marketing approach', so popular in commercial organizations, is not appropriate to a public utility. They point out that their product satisfies a basic need rather than meeting the changing requirements of a luxury market, and that the demand for their product has grown with the size and affluence of the population. Attempts to stimulate demand by advertising and publicity campaigns have had little effect.

The organization thus has relatively limited discretion and control over its output. The same is true of its inputs.

Choice of materials, and the prices paid for them, is heavily restricted by government control. The major remaining areas of freedom are the means of production and distribution.

All this is reflected in the nature of the manpower used by the organization and the career patterns within it. Jobs are of two kinds: (a) specialist posts related to the technology of its products and (b) administrative posts concerned with managing the specialists, running the distribution process and looking after the flows of funds. Careers also tend to fall into these two categories. On the one hand there is the specialist/technical career in which the man moves through a sequence of jobs requiring increasing technical competence, carrying out tasks having greater importance and responsibility attached to them. On the other hand, there is the administrative career starting at the bottom with clerical duties and moving up through supervision of sections, then departments, with responsibility for an increasing range of administrative activities. The administrative career can lead to the higher levels of the organization, whereas the technical career terminates some way below this. It is customary for a number of people who reach the top of the technical career ladder to switch to the administrative side. This provides the most commonly perceived problem of career development in the organization.

These institutional career patterns have three well-marked characteristics. First, the rungs on the various career ladders are very much formalized and have distinct labels, explicitly stated responsibilities and established salary scales. Moving up a career ladder is also highly formalized, a specified amount of experience and level of competence being required for each upward move. Secondly, most people enter the careers at the bottom. As a corollary, there are few graduates on the technical side and few people on the administrative side who have experience of working in any other organization. A third, and related, point is that few managers leave the organization. We are not sure why this should be so. The nature of the work may not fit people for work in other organizations, or at least this may appear so to the managers concerned. Perhaps this sort of organization recruits to some extent by 'self-selection', attracting people who want this kind of career and the relative certainty about the future that it provides. Alternatively, people who have invested their time and effort in making a start on this sort of a career may feel disinclined to write this off by leaving.

What then of management development? Much of what the organization considers to be management development is built into the highly explicit and formalized careers. This means reliance on job experience and particularly on experience of jobs that the person will later be supervising. In addition, steps have been taken in recent years to supplement such development by planning and implementing management development as an activity in its own right. This has been made the responsibility of a senior person in the organization. It is perhaps not surprising that the additional management development activities are taking the form of a procedure that parallels the institutional careers: formally described, universally applied throughout the organization, and comprising standard procedures to cover all the phases in its operation. This makes it possible to represent the procedure in the form of a flow chart, which can be outlined as follows:

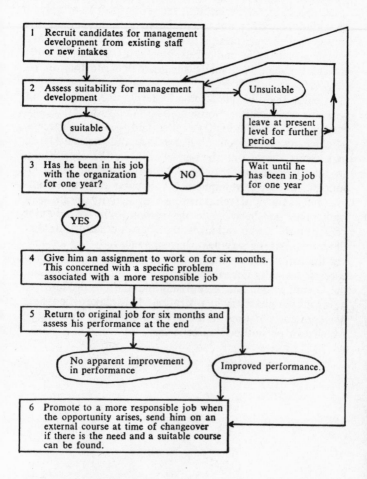

1. Recruit candidates for management development from existing staff or new intakes

2. Assess suitability for management development

    Unsuitable

    suitable

    leave at present level for further period

3. Has he been in his job with the organization for one year?

    NO

    Wait until he has been in job for one year

    YES

4. Give him an assignment to work on for six months. This concerned with a specific problem associated with a more responsible job

5. Return to original job for six months and assess his performance at the end

    No apparent improvement in performance

    Improved performance.

6. Promote to a more responsible job when the opportunity arises, send him on an external course at time of changeover if there is the need and a suitable course can be found.

Similar flow charts could be drawn up to show the details of the procedures for assessment and selection of jobs and assignments.

The procedure runs quite smoothly and seems successful in channeling more able managers into more responsible and important jobs. However, there are a number of problems:

1 It is still not possible for young able men to progress very fast into senior posts even on the management development scheme. This is because it causes too much friction with existing staff who 'have come up the hard way'.

2 Because of this it is difficult to attract highly qualified people to the organization, or to fit them in at a level with a salary and responsibilities that fit their expectations.

3 It is difficult to find suitable external courses to use in conjunction with the management development system because courses of suitable levels tend to be filled with people considerably younger than the organizations' candidates. This can be uncomfortable both for course organizers and candidates.

4 Although the assignment approach does help with the transfer from technical to administrative jobs, it does not get over the problem completely. External courses could in principle be particularly useful in smoothing the transition, but it is this sort of candidate that the organization has difficulty in placing on appropriate courses.

In summary, therefore, the management development process in this organization is carried out by the use of an explicit procedure that supplements and reinforces the established promotion following experience pattern, which runs from the bottom to the top. The result is that more able people do progress faster but not as fast as in other organizations; also, it is almost impossible to fit in the highly qualified people that privately owned commercial organizations value highly.

The Administrative Staff College, Henley

We have chosen Henley as our second example of management development in action for a number of reasons. One is that it has recently been studied in some depth by Dr R N Rapoport and colleagues from the Tavistock Institute of Human Relations, in close association with the College staff. We have leaned heavily on this excellent study in the present discussion.

The main reason for selecting Henley is that it allows us to consider an unusual and important aspect of management development. The staff at Henley have been running the main General Management Course for many years, and there has been a continued demand for places from a wide variety of organizations, in Britain and overseas. Although the course has been constantly adapting in detail to changing situations, the underlying concept has been widely recognized and remains essentially unchanged since the establishment of the College immediately after the second world war. This suggests that the course is meeting a persistent need—one that is common to managers at a particular stage in their development. Our purpose here is to consider the nature of the need that Henley meets in its management development programme.

Henley carries out other activities as well as its main General Management Course but it is for this that it is best known; our description is concerned simply with this course.

One of Dr Rapoport's major contributions to understanding Henley is his concept of it as a 'developmental community'. Such a community aims to provide a set of experiences for its temporary members, to help them to bridge a 'role discontinuity'. A role discontinuity is an abrupt change of the set of expectations of an individual by those with whom he interacts. Many promotions are formal recognitions of the fact that an individual has gradually taken on greater responsibility. In this case there is no role discontinuity: rather there has been role adaptation. However, there are some career steps that involve discontinuity rather than adaptation. The particular role discontinuity relating to Henley is that between a functional (or specialized) management and one that is concerned with general management or administration. To the extent to which experience in functional management leads to development of modes of behaviour, skills, habits of thought and action that are insufficient or inappropriate for fulfilling the expectations of a person in a general management role, there is a need for a developmental experience. Such an experience has two major components. First, there is 'role disengagement'. In any interacting set of people where a more or less stable role structure—enduring set of mutual expectations—is established there are some obvious and many subtle processes by which each individual is informed about specific current expectations, about how he currently stands, and by which sanctions and rewards are applied to foster conformity to the expectations. Role disengagement is the process of severing these links, which are necessary for role maintenance but disfunctional for change.

Secondly, there is the process of preparation for the new role, in this case general management or administration. Dr Rapoport calls this process 'the cultivation of positive role-conceptions' and it involves not only the development of a conceptual framework suitable for taking the new role effectively but also developing appropriate skills.

The major features of the main Henley General Management Course can now be described in terms of the way they contribute to these two major processes.

Role disengagement is brought about mainly because the Course is a full time residential programme, in which the participant lives and works with a number of people from many other organizations (though at each stage, most of the work is done in small groups). Not only is the participant relieved of formal interaction with colleagues, superiors and subordinates at work, but also of informal contacts at work and socially with work colleagues and others, all of whom tend to react to him in terms of his functional management role. Furthermore, the length of the Course usually requires provision to be made for each participant's job to be carried out by someone else, or by a set of other people on a temporary or permanent basis.

The necessary pre-Course process of 'handing over the job' also contributes to role disengagement.

Cultivation of *positive role-conceptions and appropriate skills* results from the subject matter and the organization of the Course. General management can be characterized as making effective policy, taking into account the factors that affect the organization as a whole, and integrating the efforts of functional specialists. A number of skills can be inferred from this. General management is likely to involve a high degree of joint decision making, consultation and persuasion, and taking responsibility for the work of functional specialists with different skills, attitudes and backgrounds. It is also likely to involve dealing with complex problems under tight constraints of time, using constantly changing and uncertain information. A suitable conceptual framework must enable the general manager to think of the organization as a whole in relation to the major pressures on it from its environment, and about its present and alternative internal organizations and procedures.

Broadly speaking, the Henley Course serves to develop these skills through practice of working in small groups, called syndicates, which study various topics. The set of topics, which represent what can be called the content or subject matter, suggest the conceptual framework.

One of the major controls that the Henley staff exert on the Course is through determining the composition of the syndicates which form the main working units throughout the Course. To give the participants practice in some of the above skills, the syndicates are mixed in terms of both type of organization that the participants are affiliated to and also the functional specialisms in which they have experience. When selecting participants for the Course, the staff therefore maintain a balance between industrial, commercial and financial organizations, nationalized industries, Civil Service, trade unions, local authorities, HM Forces and participants from overseas organizations. The aim is to produce a 'miniature course' within each syndicate group. A member of the directing staff is attached to each syndicate but the syndicate members largely organize themselves to study the various topics; the chairmanship is rotated around the group so that everyone has a turn. Directing staff advise and play an important part in preparing and making available information relevant to the topics. Frequently, work on topics culminates in plenary sessions in which the syndicate chairmen present the conclusions of their groups and there is a general discussion. The syndicates are re-mixed for a few of the topics so that the participants benefit from interaction with a wider range of people. There are also a number of supporting activities in the form of visitors and visits, seminars on economics, analytical concepts and techniques, and preliminary accounts and statistics.

The subject matter or content of the course at the time of the Rapoport study was organized under six main headings:

1 Survey of organizational structures
2 Internal organization and administration
3 External relations
4 The enterprise in action
5 Britain and the international community
6 Power and responsibility

Historical development

The guiding concepts of main General Management Courses have changed very little since Henley was founded in 1945. This may well be because the aim was clearly seen from the start as providing experience to develop the participants from people competent in their chosen field into people capable of overall and general responsibility. The general method of the course, centred on syndicate work, was designed with the experiences of the armed forces staff colleges in mind. Minor adjustments have been made to the size and composition of the syndicates and a number of extra activities have been added, such as the seminars on analytical techniques.

Similarly, the content of the course has developed

incrementally, without any major revision. The changes have been made in response to observable changes in the world. For example, there is more attention now to the international business scene than there was when multi-national organizations were less common; since the development of computers and managerial techniques, the course includes more relevant material, some of it systematically taught.

In general, however, the picture is one of relative stability, suggesting that Henley is satisfying an enduring need.

The effects of Henley

Many interesting conclusions have come out of Dr Rapoport's study of ex-Henley members, only a few of which can be discussed here.

First, the benefits of the course as perceived by nominators and participants were broadly speaking consistent with the interpretation of Henley as a developmental community. Nominators tended to use phrases like 'stretched', 'broadened', 'taken the blinkers off' to describe the effect on participants. The participants themselves valued the interactive experiences in the seminar groups, which they found particularly useful in giving them less stereotyped views of other organizations, allowing them to consider their own more objectively and increasing their self-esteem. There were also demands for more input of expertise from the staff. To some extent this is a legitimate request, given the newly developed techniques useful in management and the course has adapted to this new need. Some requests of this sort may be the result of the stresses of role disengagement and acquiescence to these could be disfunctional.

Secondly, there is evidence that the course has been successful. Those participants whom the staff judged as being most developed were shown in the follow-up to be those who went further in general management careers. Furthermore, the follow-up study showed that there were distinguishably different patterns of career development amongst the managers attending Henley. The three major types of pattern detected were named 'metamorphs', 'incrementalists' and 'tangentialists'. Metamorphs progress their careers in large, rather discontinuous steps which often, though not necessarily, entail a change in organization. As the name suggests, incrementalists progress by more continuous steps, following more firmly established career routes within organizations. Tangentialists tend to occupy jobs that involve much contact outside the organization, and their careers develop as they move to other organizations through their contacts, or as their area of concern becomes more central to the organizations they are already in. Managers with these different career patterns had correspondingly different views about the Course. Although there is no suggestion that Henley was more or less suitable for the different types of managers, this difference does raise the general question, which applies to all general management courses, of whether different types of course fit better with different types of manager.

Lastly, there was some evidence from the follow-up of the course participants that, where development was not followed by an actual transfer to a role of a more general management nature, the development as a manager was displaced into effort put into non-work activities or diverted by a process of moving to another organization.

Management development in an international company

Our third example of management development in action must place the emphasis on 'action', because any attempt to catch the rapidly changing realities of management development in the company must inevitably lag behind the current position. First, it should be emphasized that members of the company's top management have deliberately chosen this mode of development, believing it to be more appropriate to the needs of the organization than a centrally imposed set of standard personnel procedures.

This decision does not mean abdication of responsibility for top management involvement in management development: the chairman is more than usually personally involved in development activities and has given the matter special mention in several successive annual reports.

Before describing what must be just a sample of the management development activities going on, a brief description must be given of the company's structure. It has four major divisions, each with considerable autonomy, linked by a relatively small central management team. Decentralization does not stop at the level of these four major groupings but also applies broadly speaking within them, being carried through to the sub-divisional level and to the operating units within these sub-divisions. This degree of decentralization has been brought about gradually over a number of years as a matter of deliberate policy. In this process most of the services that had been dealt with centrally were split. Education and training was an exception to this rule, reflecting the top management view of the importance of this function. Nevertheless, the training function has been radically changed in the decentralization process. In the case of management development, the centre now has two roles. First, the top management in the central function is deeply involved in ensuring that the most senior positions in the parts and divisions of the company are occupied by competent people and that this will continue. In doing this the centre is attempting to set an example of how managers should be developed by their line superiors, with the support and assistance of specialists. Secondly, the centre supports divisions by providing management and supervisory courses for defined needs and by providing 'resource' people who work on special problems throughout the organization where payoffs in terms of management development, organization development and immediate problem-solving may occur together.

Courses, or rather development programmes, are run for all levels of management, including the top divisional men. In this latter case the top managers in the central organization are deeply concerned in the selection for, operation and follow up of the development programmes which are organized around line case studies from the company and real life projects investigating actual aspects of its operation.

The senior functional specialists in training and education participate in the top management development programmes, and work with the top managers on the appointment of senior divisional personnel. They also oversee the provision of courses and other assistance with management development for lower levels in the divisions. Although the central training and education function has potentially considerable influence over divisions through their involvement in the selection of top divisional managers, it does not use it, for example, to impose standardized procedures for assessment and training throughout the organization. Instead, the divisions are encouraged to be active in developing their managers to be experimental in the approaches they use and to fit their approaches to the particular requirements of their divisions.

A programme of management courses is one form of assistance which the central department of manpower and training makes available. These courses are provided as a service for the various parts of the organization to use at their own discretion and on the same basis as outside courses. They are designed to meet the organization's needs and every opportunity is taken to ensure that they are used as a part of planned management development activities. The director of these courses takes four types of information into account in planning courses:

the training needs revealed by the various management assessment procedures used in various parts of the organization; a questionnaire on training needs completed by training officers working in different parts of the organization; the reactions of those participating in the courses; the information gathered in following up course members and in contacts made for other purposes.

In this way every effort is made to keep the courses relevant to the requirements of 'backbone managers'—a phrase from the Mant Report which the company finds highly relevant to its own experiences. Effort is also devoted to meeting the other Mant Report criticisms of training practice. People coming on courses are encouraged to discuss the reasons for attendance with their superiors, to be committed to the exercise, and to use what they learn. A number of follow-up activities are designed with course participants and their bosses.

The courses provided in this way are well used, but it is recognized that they do not in themselves constitute management development and that they will continue only as long as they are found useful by line managers, who are regarded as responsible for the development of their subordinates.

We have already indicated the impossibility of describing all the management development activities in such a large and decentralized organization. Brief examples from two of the divisions must serve to give an idea of the variety of activities and approaches.

In the first of the divisions to be considered, the senior training and development man is a strong believer in matching the organization of the management development function to that of the business. Much of his effort goes into developing and running procedures of assessing managers and keeping a career register of general managers. The method of assessment he encourages is one in which superiors assess subordinates in consultation with them, along the lines of management by objectives, although not making full use of the MBO approach. Superior—subordinate discussions and similar discussions among other groupings on objectives, standards, performances and other MBO topics are seen as a major training medium. He uses the services of the centre, including the courses, just like any other outside resource and is trying out a number of other management development activities. The managing director of the division has followed the lead of head office and initiated a development programme for his senior subordinates in which he is actively involved and which focuses on actual divisional problems.

The second division is characterized by several operating units. In one, the heads of each of the 13 sub-units are regarded as responsible for management development within these sub-units. In a situation where financial performance is given high priority, the training officer believes it to be his job to ensure that management development is given sufficient attention. He spends much time discussing training needs in the units, and finds that the major requirement is for specific training to deal with specific problems. For this reason he encourages the use of central courses only when their relevance is clearly established. In the past the unit has used some Blake Managerial Grid Training, which is seen as having brought about real changes in effecting more openness in communications and the effective use of people. However, the training officer now considers that this can be achieved at less expense by their own efforts.

The other operating unit covers a major growth area of the company's activities. The man responsible for management development in this division faces the problem of getting the management resources which will allow the division to grow at the desired rate. He has a centralized management development function because he sees the need for an overall view and a plan to deal with the demands of growth. There is a firm belief in this unit that the major need for effective management is a thorough and intimate knowledge of all levels of the specific business of the unit, and that this is best learnt through experience. The major strategy of management development is therefore one of visits, secondments and job rotation. Existing management has been systematically surveyed for potential; graduates and experienced managers are also recruited and developed through the job rotation approach.

In summary, the development of the company's most senior managers is dealt with centrally; the remaining responsibility is delegated to the parts and divisions, where central services are offered but are not imposed on them.

The three brief examples show that this responsibility really is delegated, because these divisions and operating units have been able to develop their own approaches and, in particular, to decide for themselves whether to delegate management development further down the system or to centralize it at their own level. There is no doubt that this has allowed the various parts to develop individual approaches, appropriate to their own circumstances, and that many opportunities exist for similar further development.

In conclusion

These examples of management development at the level of organizations and institutions bring out the contrasts in ways of thinking about management development which we found in our analysis of the metaphors. The public utility, with high standards of reliability and service to maintain, within an area of operations which is largely determined for it and protected from competition, is concerned with managers as a stable resource and seeks to guarantee their continued supply and quality. For this reason it was possible to describe the management development activities of this organization by means of the sort of flow process chart widely used in engineering and building construction activities. On the other hand, the international company, with its complex and dynamically developing business is more concerned with managers as resourceful people. It recognizes that many of the factors determining development are outside the control of the official management developers. Metaphors of the forest and the jungle and the military seem more appropriate. Just as the metaphors bring out a middle ground between the extremes, so the 'developmental community' of the Henley Staff College, though it has military implications, aspires after a balance of qualities, of individual and personal responsibility within an organizational and social context. On the whole its supportive character seems to bring it close to the agricultural metaphor.

Fascinating though the study of metaphors and case studies can be, a time comes when one looks away from them. After all, their task is to illuminate reality. Metaphors are homely, practical devices of everyday thought—rough maps of an area of experience or observation. To some extent, we have violated their simplicity by anatomizing them. But we hope that the way is now open for us to move beyond the metaphors used by practising managers, and from case studies, to a somewhat more formal, systematic approach for thinking about management development. We shall dignify it with the label of 'model', to indicate that it is rather more self-conscious and improvable than a metaphor (though we are reminded of a colleague at Manchester Business School who complained that nowadays every diagram is called a model).

3 Thinking about management development: A simple model

So far, we have distinguished between two approaches underlying the metaphors commonly used by managers when they discuss management development and which make sense of the approaches to management development of contrasting organizations. First, there is the view that managers are stable resources purchased by the organization for a specific purpose; secondly, that managers are resourceful people who use their intelligence, initiative, and energies to the best advantage of the organization without losing an interest in their own advancement. This two-fold distinction roughly matches the division in most organizations between the maintenance of steady states, and the handling of discontinuities of one form or another. The two most commonly observable forms of discontinuity are (i) handling breakdowns in day to day working and (ii) planning and implementing major changes in the activities of the organization.

We shall now set about building a simple model that will give us some useful guidelines to classifying the main forms of management development, and will show that confusions can easily arise around the varied uses of the term 'development'. Four terms are necessary for the model: *development drama, breakdown drama, ritual and routine*. Starting with routine, this is the class of managerial activities concerned with maintaining steady states, where the ends to be attained and the means of attaining them are, broadly speaking, known in advance. Development drama covers all those changes that represent a major improvement (or intended improvement) in the activities of the organization. The term 'drama' appears to be appropriate because the organization is moving into a new situation and is not able to anticipate all the contingencies that are likely to arise. There may be an element of planning and this will bring the drama closer to the level of routine, to the extent of which the planning is effective. In an extreme case an actual change may be so thoroughly pre-planned that the change, when it at last occurs, becomes almost an anti-climax. Where this happens, we can say that the drama has been gradually turned into a routine by the process of planning. A breakdown drama is dramatic in quite a different sense. It represents a failure in the steady flow of routine activities. It attracts a good deal of attention and mobilizes a great deal of energy for getting back to normal working. Not all breakdowns are dramas. Some of them may be so predictable that they can be corrected by standardized repair activities which themselves become routines (it is the ability of a trained mechanic or technician to engage in these rapid, almost unthinking, repairs that strikes the layman as so impressive). Somewhere between these relatively automatic 'routines' and the two kinds of dramas, one finds activities that are neither drama nor routine. Rituals, as we term this intermediate category, are neither drama nor routine.

To bring out the relationships between these four categories, a diagram may be useful.

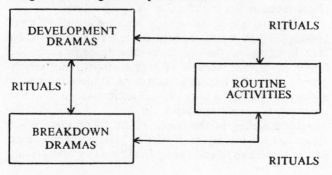

The two-way arrows merely bring out the fact of inter-action between the categories. We cannot find a more appropriate place for the category of 'ritual' than on the arrows themselves, because in this model the role of ritual is to act as a kind of bridge between the more extreme categories. In some cases, the transition from routine to drama, or from development drama to breakdown drama, may be so rapid (as with the classic 'spanner in the works') that there is not time for a ritual to mediate between drama and routine. But when the transition occurs more slowly, as happens very often in the 'running down' of a drama into a routine, or the formal preparation for a drama one knows is about to happen (the night before the battle, the building-up of energies for a hunt), then a ritual typically takes place.

Because this intermediate category is less clear-cut, by its position in our conceptual scheme, than either drama or routine, it may be valuable to comment on it now before developing it later in more detail.

Many people, especially in management, are inclined to think of ritual as a religious rather than a managerial concept. On hearing the word, their minds go to such examples as weddings, funerals, Holy Communion, or perhaps to national occasions such as Trooping the Colour or Armistice Day. If they use the term at all in connection with their own practical concerns, it is in a pejorative way. Thus productivity bargaining or other exercises in industrial relations may be condemned as 'useless rituals'. Other terms might be 'charade' or 'play-acting'.

Our own use of the concept is closer to that of social anthropologists, whose work in the last 20 years or so has been bringing out the enormous importance in traditional forms of human society of well-accepted and clearly-defined ways of handling transitions from one state to another, especially a state of high excitement to a level of everyday life and vice-versa. In many of the so-called 'simpler societies' in the Pacific or in Africa these rituals characterize every aspect of life: in building houses, making tools, preparing and eating food, meeting and greeting other people, going on journeys, dealing with joyful or painful experiences. It seems that the natural condition of man in such societies is that of ritual.

In modern society, the close association of man and machine, and the use of the machine as the standard of effective, routine performance, has tended to push the normal condition to one of routine. Since we are concerned here with management development in all its varied forms rather than with management itself, we shall now look at the ways in which management development has been expressed in these three modes of drama, ritual and routine.

Management development as routine

This strategy of management development has been widely supported and developed by many large personnel departments and also by the Industrial Training Boards. Not surprisingly, the existence of a well developed personnel department encourages the systematic analysis of management jobs, especially those that have a high degree of technical content and are at a relatively junior level in the organization. Once one comes to analyse one of the more formal kinds of management positions, it quickly becomes apparent that the procedures in such jobs have much in common with those of supervisory or even technological jobs. As a result, controlled systems can be devised for assessing effectiveness in these parts of managerial work and they become formally established as time goes on.

Large and complex organizations often welcome this process of 'rationalizing' managerial work as they find that this greatly eases the task of grading and evaluating managerial staff. The result is that management is seen from an increasingly routine point of view, as a definable combination of information, technical skills and the personal qualities that enable these to be effectively used (such as persistance, orderliness, conscientiousness).

Once the combination of required characteristics has been determined, it becomes possible to institute formal programmes of training aimed at developing these characteristics in suitably motivated individuals. We are all familiar with these programmes, which start off with clear objectives and often take the form of systematic inputs of information, systematic training and techniques of analysis and decision-making, and practice in applying the various established procedures of organization to a variety of relevant cases.

This approach, for all its strengths, has obvious weaknesses when it comes to looking at the role of the manager in bringing about change, and in dealing resourcefully with breakdowns. At this point, the systematic procedures of management development, organized by the personnel department, tend to give way to more individual and informal methods of management development controlled by line management and especially by top managers.

The most accurate label to give to the routine form of management development is surely *management training*. In training, one knows not only what is to be achieved but how to achieve it. The means and the end are both clear-cut. It is unfortunate that the term 'training' has been used in a rather slipshod way to refer to virtually any kind of learning programme. Similarly, the term 'management development', with its implications of a wide-ranging improvement in overall effectiveness, is given to narrowly conceived programmes in which the manager is acquiring routine ways of performing in particular situations.

Management development as drama

The previous strategy of management development stresses the theme of continuity in a person's development within an organization. But continuity does not enable us to handle breakdowns except those which themselves can be clearly anticipated and solved as a matter of routine. More substantial breakdowns require some kind of problem-solving approach, which involves a manager in the use of very different skills from those that enable him to maintain a steady state. Similarly, the resourceful seizing of opportunity (which itself may only be fleeting) requires qualities of perception and initiative which are by no means to be taken for granted, especially in managers trained to handle well established routines.

To those practising managers who want to see how their young subordinates work under stress, both 'opportunities' and 'problems' present the golden opportunities of a natural test-situation. The manager who has acquitted himself well in handling a steady state can be put under load by being put in charge of a new activity (opening a new branch, setting up a new plant, selling in a new market). Or he may be given a trouble-shooting assignment. These are only two types of possible changes of responsibility. In every case, the manager's seniors believe that a move of this kind will enable him to show that he has qualities that fit him for a place at the top—drive, determination, incisiveness, flair, courage, ingenuity. This can be a risky business for the man who is thrown in at the deep end. The new job can make him but it may also break him. This is the stuff of which successful careers in senior management are often made, especially those who arrive early at the top. It is also the raw material of company history, that strange mixture of myths, legends and reality that deals in heroes and villains, saints and sinners, victims and beneficiaries, rather than in faceless men and women who never rise above their station.

So far, we have focussed on dramas as discontinuities in the organization. But the term 'discontinuity' raises the question of who experiences a situation as discontinuous. A manager who moves from one well-established post to another may well find this a discontinuity, even though both jobs are part of the continuing life of the organization. At the other extreme, a manager may make a very successful career as a trouble-shooter, in which case he establishes a kind of continuity in dealing with organizational discontinuities (official receivers, firemen, venture managers and organizational consultants—are all in their different ways the beneficiaries of discontinuity).

Looking at discontinuity and therefore at drama from the point of view of individuals rather than organizations, it seems that three elements in a situation make them dramatic for the individuals who are experiencing them. These elements can be summarized as uncertainty, importance, and commitment. The situation is dramatic if the outcome of a situation, or the means by which the outcome can be secured, are unclear; if the outcome is important to the individual; and if he is committed to continuing with the situation as it develops. Clearly, each of these elements is a matter of degree and the relationship between them seems to be multiplicative rather than additive. These elements clearly depend on the relationship between each individual and a given situation, which is why so much of everyday life is tragi-comic. What is a matter of indifference to one manager may be a tragedy for another (the man who got axed), and a comedy for the third (the man who got his job).

The individuality of people's responses to the 'same' situation does not make a complete nonsense of looking at situations as dramas in their own right, because in every form of social life there are agreements on the 'definition' of situations. Thus the winding-up of a company would be generally regarded as an unfortunate affair, though it would be readily recognized that some managers may benefit from the event. In much the same way, a funeral is conventionally a sad occasion, though the heir to the fortune of the dear departed may be excused for thinking otherwise.

In management development, each person may vary somewhat in his response to the planned or unplanned discontinuities into which he is precipitated by events or by his seniors. But we can still see these discontinuities as dramatic in general terms, and thus preserve some stability in our discussion of them. Nevertheless, it may well be due to this conceptual complexity in thinking about dramas that we have so little systematic consideration of dramatic forms of management development. Management development (or as we would prefer to call it—management training) is well documented on the level of routine. But management development as drama has been left almost wholly to the world of the arts and entertainment. Television series (*The Troubleshooters*), films (*Executive Suite*) and particularly novels (*Room at the Top, The Man in the Grey Flannel Suit*) have found rich fare in dramatic representations of management and management development. Perhaps the great popularity of Robert Townsend's lively book *Up the Organization!*, with its vigorous denunciations of all routinized activities (including management training), is owed largely to its bringing drama out of fiction and into fact (though the fact seems often indistinguishable from fiction).

A more systematic study of top management selection and development, based on interviews with senior management in 13 American companies by Albert Glickman and colleagues from the American Institutes for Research, shows that even in large organizations the senior managers work closely together, rather like members of a small company. They looked for men who made an impact on their surroundings and showed the ability to make hard decisions and live with them.

There seems no clear evidence as yet that breakdown dramas are a better route to the top than development dramas (to take a specific example—making an unprofitable unit profitable as compared with making a profitable unit even more profitable). The 'hearsay' of management discussion on the most successful paths to senior management seems evenly divided between two apparently opposing bits of folk wisdom—'always take care to be associated with success' and 'whoever follows a failure always gains by the contrast'.

In discussing management development by routine, we suggested that the systematic process of developing routine effectiveness (even when the routines are highly complex and advanced) should be called management *training*. But the development of effectiveness in handling drama, which calls on many qualities other than skill—qualities of character—seems to be a very full development of the manager as a person. In some cases he may not be a very pleasant kind of person, and this raises questions of approach and morality that the business of training tends to leave on one side.

In our view, management development in the fullest sense is concerned with the experience of development dramas and breakdown dramas, particularly development dramas. Whatever the present position may be in gaining senior management experience, there seems little doubt that the experience of handling opportunities has many advantages over dealing with problems. As usually encountered, problems of breakdown are pre-occupied with re-establishing the *status quo*. The methods that an energetic and imaginative manager uses in dealing with breakdowns may be a source of fascination, even inspiration, to the observer. But they are bound within a closed system, whereas opportunities take the manager into a world of unforeseen possibilities.

It may be a sign of impoverished imagination that so many managers see opportunities as a problem, a grim obligation laid on the managers of organizations rather than a splendid move into the unknown. Even the language that one uses in speaking of opportunities has been so caustically handled that one hesitates to use the words except with defensive irony or apology: 'challenge', 'adventure', 'unforeseen', 'creative'. How much more accustomed we have been to passive constructions such as 'pressure', 'force of circumstances', 'demands of the environment' and 'difficulties'. One feels that with a future like this, all one can do is to give in or pray!

Management development as ritual

Between the dramas and the routines of management development and management training lie the innumerable half-way houses of management rituals. We have already tried to establish this concept in the anthropological sense, seeing it as a middle ground between the uniqueness and discontinuity of drama and the smooth-running, habitual flow of routines. Even if the full implications of the concept of ritual have not yet been fully grasped, one can readily see that many of the more formal kinds of management development programmes are ritual in form. They do not take place often enough to be routines (for the participants, that is, and it is they after all who are the aim of the exercise). Yet they are not really dramas, because the trappings of such courses stress their rationality and predictability.

The lengthy residential courses provided by business schools are a case in point. They take a manager from his familiar environment and face him, among a group of his fellows, with a series of challenges: business games, role-playing exercises, case discussion, syndicate work. Some of these are very real in the sense that decisions have to be made, positions have to be defended and time is always pressing. But the whole stream of activities takes place in a setting in which a moment's reflection suggests to the participants that 'it has all happened before'. The course is one of a series, perhaps number 20 or even 117, and the programme precisely establishes each activity, however gripping, within a pre-determined schedule.

Such programmes are also widely used within industry, in industrial staff colleges and management education centres. Here the rituals can come a little closer to home: inspiriting addresses by the members of one's board of directors or cases derived from one's organization (we recall one international seminar run by a multi-national firm in which a senior manager, with a shock, discovered that he appeared as a leading figure in a case drawn from his own firm, mercifully protected by an 'alias'.)

What makes these activities rituals rather than dramas or routines? They are rituals because they are set apart from the ordinary flow of life in the organization, in a strange middle ground between the calm efficiency of a routine and the powerful unfamiliarity and heightened reality of drama. A drama is memorable: it only occurs once, for good or ill. Rituals are more familiar. They draw their strength from drama: the cases used by business schools were once slices of life, now cooled to ritual status (in the right hands, they can recover some of their primal fire).

We cannot, of course, assert that nothing in the programmes can attain the standing of a drama. Obviously, a serious breakdown in the effectiveness of the programme can be genuinely dramatic, as some tyro programme directors have found to their cost. More unusually, a course can develop its own reality, drawn from the challenge of the programme or the aspirations of the participants. The management programmes of some of the leading American business schools, with their competitiveness, their ruthless demands for high levels of achievement and their high failure-rates, have been compared to marine battle courses or even to the battle itself.

On the theme of ritual, Charles Handy, Professor of Management Development at the London Business School, has suggested that many courses for experienced managers perform the function of conferring public recognition on the manager who is 'sent', a state of organizational grace that he terms 'the accolade effect'. He believes that it often has the unfortunate effect of unintentionally providing course members with excellent reasons for refusing to learn anything from the programme of work, since they believe that they are already designated as established successes and have nothing further to acquire than a surface glitter.

There seems to be a natural affinity between rituals and education, just as there is a relationship between routines and training. Rituals are close to values, they are linked with dramas and not only with routines. Education too must draw from real life if it is not to run down into an empty shell of routines, all the more dreary for being purely repetitive rather than useful. By 'real life' here is meant something more than the flow of everyday activities outside the school or college. We mean 'real' in the sense of being especially meaningful or significant.

Just as the television or film 'Western' manages to survive as a ritual after hundreds of repetitions, because of the myths of courage and individual sacrifice that are embodied in the genre, so the courses that remind their participants (implicity rather than explicitly) that they are members of a noble profession, or a decent and self-respecting company, manage to touch an enduring nerve.

These considerations suggest that rituals are not merely a transitional stage between dramas and routines, inherently unstable (though this can be true of some rituals), but can be a stable balance of extremes, with a connective and even integrative function. In situations of social conflict, for example, a ritual 'middle term' can be of great and enduring influence. We have only to instance the industrial mediator, the judge or a referee in a sporting contest.

Rituals can thus range between wide extremes, from a phase that an activity passes through on its way from a novel response to a habit, to a powerful form of mediation and control. This latter sense of the term seems to be of particular significance for management education, and it seems no accident that the Administrative Staff College at Henley has developed a programme that is very sensitive to ritual in this deeper sense. The emphasis on the sharing of experience, the disengagement from one's current responsibilities, the sustained opportunity to reflect, in beautiful surroundings, on the wider responsibilities of management, and the detailed consideration of biographies of outstanding leaders: all seem to be mediating between the dramas of organizational leadership and the routine effectiveness of well-managed systems.

In conclusion

We began this chapter with the observation that the metaphors used by practising managers to describe management development are expressions of two underlying themes: managers as stable resources of the organization employing them and managers as resourceful people, dealing with various kinds of discontinuity. The 'model' developed in this chapter has divided management activities into four groups: development dramas, routines, breakdown dramas and rituals. Management development can be seen from three points of view: *training* for routine effectiveness, *education* for effective balancing and co-ordination in the 'middle ground' or organizational life and *development* for the resourceful handling of development and breakdown dramas.

4 Developing managerial effectiveness

Operations management, development management and general management

A theme that has constantly recurred throughout our discussion so far is the contrast between stability and change. We saw this first in the form of stable human resources and resourceful adaptable people. Then we expressed this contrast between people as a contrast between two kinds of activities—dramas and routines. Now it reappears in the contrast between two kinds of management, which we shall call *operations management and development management*.

In real life, operations management is a complicated mix of steady states, breakdown dramas and connecting rituals. Development management is essentially 'the management of innovation'. Innovation is useless unless it can be turned at some stage into effective operations, and we expect in real life to find complex connections between operations and development.

Despite this complexity, one can distinguish between operations and development. Even though vulnerable to breakdown, operations are always *aspiring* to become routines. Development reaches into the future and only loops back into a routine after it has taken in something new and strange. It has then succeeded in establishing a new routine. The distinction between operations and development has been neatly put by Stafford Beer (who has done outstanding pioneering work in establishing and developing this terminology) as that between 'inside and now' and 'outside and the future'. 'Inside', in the sense used here, is not only limited to production but also includes production sales, distribution and so on, because these are inside the firm's present sphere of operations. 'Outside' means outside this current sphere but still actually or potentially relevant, such as the people one is not yet employing but may be able to use for some future activity, the skills one has not yet acquired but could learn if necessary, and products which the firm is not yet producing (but might be well able to manage) for markets which have not yet been established. Since there is clearly an enormous number of different matters that are outside even the largest organization, the managers of the development function have the difficult and important task of deciding which are relevant to the interests of the organization, not as it is now but as it could be.

The whole flavour of management development in the operations sector of an organization tends to be different from that in the development sector. Operations have a stronger sense of discipline (one might say that it is merely a strong sense of reality), growing out of the tight technical and economic constraints within which they are required to work. They are handling 'hardware' rather than ideas. In development activity there is often a longer time-perspective, more difficulty in stating what the precise objectives are to be, and much more need for self-confidence on the part of the manager than in the operations sector, where there is tangible evidence of effectiveness and well-established precedents to follow. In the development field, individuality tends to be a virtue; in operations, it may be viewed as an eccentricity.

This is one of the reasons why some mediation and control of the relationship between development and operations is necessary. This activity fits well with what we see as the nature of general management.

Putting it at the simplest, general management has two key tasks: (i) inside the organization, to co-ordinate development management and operations management, and

(ii) outside the organization, to manage the relationships with governing systems (that is, government and other organizations more powerful than the organization currently being managed).

There seems to be a good deal of evidence that general management in Britain has been backward in its efforts to bring together the development function and the operations function. This may be because British management has been highly traditional in its attitudes and experience, being made up mainly of highly experienced operations managers, some of whom have had painful experience in handling major breakdowns. Development is seen as an area of high risk and therefore high cost: an aspect of management to keep as far distant as possible. Relations with government and other powerful groups have also been somewhat neglected. When using the simple model developed in the previous chapter, we can see that an effective general management will have skills in all four areas of management: development dramas, breakdown dramas, managing steady states and, above all, the integrative rituals that bring all these effectively together.

In the remainder of this chapter, we shall focus on the requirements of development management because the practice of management development has been most seriously retarded in this area. In the examples referred to at the beginning of these notes, the public utility is much more representative of British firms than is the international company. Nevertheless, in discussing the fostering of effective 'development managers', one can hardly avoid looking constantly at the relationships between development and operations. This becomes apparent immediately we set out to look at the varieties of development management that have already emerged

The varieties of development management

If a wise and far-sighted general manager were to set up a viable development function, we would no doubt give close attention to the effectiveness of this function in detecting opportunities and translating them into a form that could be responded to constructively by the people in the operational sector of the organization. He would not wish to impose the development function on a busy, possibly embattled and reluctant operations function by the use of authority: he would want the relationship between the two vital parts of the organization to be mutually rewarding. He would be greatly concerned about the skill and energy of his key development managers but would also think carefully about their structure.

When one looks at organizations that have been involved in consistent development work, it is unusual to find a coherent development sector, conceivably because of an unfortunate lack of wisdom and far-sightedness, at any level of management. What has happened is that the basic operational functions have 'grown' their own development sections or departments, and have tended to keep these under close operating control. This may be a special case of a more general point made by Paul Lawrence and Jay Lorsch of Harvard. They show that organizations tend to develop differentiated parts to match the special requirements of the environment within which the organization has to survive. Thus, the need to purchase raw materials produces a purchasing function, the need to find a purchaser for one's goods or services fosters a sales function. These specialized parts of the organization can become so sharply divided that they are in danger of splitting off altogether. This requires an integrative function to keep the organization coherent and effective at whatever level of wholeness is required for survival.

Since an organization is made up of sub-systems, the same process of mutual adaptation can also be seen within. Since the well-established operational functions provide the internal 'environment' for the development function, one sees clear signs of functional relationships growing up. Perhaps the two most clearly marked development functions are marketing and research-and-development. Marketing links up with sales and distribution while research-and-development links up with production. There are growing signs in Britain of a 'development finance' function emerging to scan the financial environment for opportunities, with special reference to effective programmes of future loans and investment. This links with accounting and the financing of established operations, both of which are clearly part of the operations sector of the organization.

Two more sets of links, rather more ill-defined in most cases, are those between operational research and technical services, on the one hand, and between personnel and 'organizational development', on the other. The purchasing function has been relatively ill-developed in Britain and does not seem to have, as yet, any kind of analogue in the area of development management.

It is noticeable that many organizations, especially those with close control of expenditure, move into development activities extremely cautiously, and often sub-contract the relevant work to consulting firms, or specialized agencies such as merchant banks, industry-wide research and development bodies or even universities. Only when the possibility of making a contribution has become evident is a development section in the relevant area brought into the organization itself (often, alas, as an isolated and vulnerable individual: a behavioural scientist, a market research specialist, an economic or technological forecaster or even a corporate planner).

The various operational functions are brought into some kind of unity, however reluctant, by the technological, economic and market constraints of everyday life. Unfortunately, the diverse development functions often spring apart and the tendency in British industry to starve the development sector of resources (often through grim necessity rather than deliberate choice) has encouraged a miserable battle for the crumbs falling from the operations managers' table. The resulting spectacle of research and development against marketing, operational research against organizational development (the personnel variant, at least), and finance against all, has been a depressing example of the fierce divisiveness of the impoverished.

A major task of the development function, in coming years, will be to bring its specialized activities together, without threatening the effectiveness of their ties with the operational activities. A well-managed development sector can make sure that sensitivity to the environment is not sacrificed to internal conflicts.

The expansion of our model from its first simple state, reasonably close to some homely managerial metaphors, to its present distinctly controversial presentation of the varieties of development management may have been confusing. The accompanying diagram attempts to set out the relationships as clearly as possible as an aid to further discussion.

MANAGERIAL ACTIVITIES

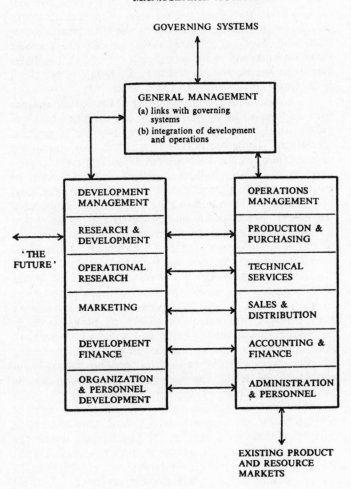

A major change from the first outline of the model is the emergence of general management as a vital integrative function, relating the activities of development to those of maintaining the organization on an even keel and of handling breakdowns effectively. The fact that this central function is linked in the model with rituals rather than with development dramas brings out the complex status of ritual within the model as a concept that includes mediation and regulation, and not only modes of transition from dramas to routines and vice versa.

A second change is the grouping of breakdown dramas with routines to form the category of operations management, which we divided into the familiar functional specialisms. These are not, of course, the only specialized divisions in operating management. One often finds division into regions, into production groups and into types of market (other than geographical areas, which are the basis of regions). To have added these would have complicated the model unmanageably and obscured the tendency that we have described for development activities to grow out of the functional specialisms of production, selling, personnel, accounting/finance and technical services.

Although the model is still rather complicated, it has thereby gained in realism. One does not find programmes in 'development drama' in business schools or company staff colleges. But there are plenty of programmes in marketing, operational research and investment appraisal. And there are a growing number of programmes aiming to encourage what is called the 'general management approach', of seeing the specialisms in relation to the overall requirements of the organization.

This is a convenient point to return to the different approaches of management development. Our attempt to categorize them as drama, ritual and routine served the purpose of clarifying these concepts rather than of describing management training, education and development in terms which people professionally engaged in these activities would readily recognize. If we start from the approaches that can be seen to be embodied in management development centres such as business schools, independent institutions such as Henley, company staff colleges and training centres, there seem to be at least six distinguishable ways of tackling the job of developing managerial effectiveness.

Approaches to management training, education and development

We used to think of these approaches as 'strategies', using a prestigious term from the military metaphor. But this perhaps implies something more specific than the more subjective set of intentions and decision rules we have in mind. Managers responsible for development programmes rarely think the matter through as a considered strategy, chosen from available alternatives in relation to overall objectives and relevant resources. This is hardly surprising since, like other managers, they have been under tremendous pressure to provide a continuing flow of programmes (usually in the form of courses) with little opportunity to engage in reflection, let alone revolution.

The six approaches (found in a complicated mixture within any single programme) are:

1 Attempting to provide an opportunity for looking at the *background of management activities*. This might be called 'setting the scene' or 'opening windows of new horizons'. The introduction of ideas and material from academic disciplines such as economics, sociology, psychology and mathematics can be relevant to this approach.

2 Providing an opportunity for managers to learn *rigorous techniques of analysis and decision* in relatively clear-cut situations (for example, techniques of linear programming, discounted cash flow, appraisal of personnel performance).

3 Providing an opportunity of learning about the *functional requirements of a specialist job* within the organization. This may range from an 'appreciation' programme giving a broad understanding of functions other than one's own (the main object being to persuade managers that other functions are necessary), to an attempt to gain mastery of a particular specialist function.

4 Developing greater effectiveness in seeing problems from a *general management point of view* (sometimes the business school labels of 'business policy' or 'corporate strategy' are used here).

5 Providing experienced managers with an opportunity of *sharing experience* by focussing upon areas of common interest, either as opportunities or problems.

6 Enabling managers *to work on opportunities or problems,* to make recommendations and to manage their implementation in the context of the organization.

The first five approaches are a mixture of training and education, fitting well with our earlier discussion of management development as routine and ritual. The second is largely training and there are substantial elements of training in the third. The rest are mainly educational, at least in the form that is usually adopted (for example, business policy and corporate strategy are taught through cases and complex analytical and decision-making techniques; and sharing experience—though potentially dramatic—often becomes sociable and diffuse 'discussion').

The approach that looks at opportunities and problems, and actually works on them, shifts the focus from training and education to development of managerial effectiveness in actual managerial situations. To be fair to the courses on general management, and some of those on functional specialisms, there is often an attempt to gain effectiveness by using business games and other methods that simulate real situations. This brings a fusion, in some cases, of these approaches with the sixth, which we now want to examine in greater detail.

Learning by discovery

The distinction that is being made in the concepts of training, education and development is essentially one of the kind of learning that takes place. In training, a systematic programme is followed by a person under instruction, the aim of which is to enable him to achieve a specified level of competence. In development, the achievement of competence cannot be programmed in the same way, because the ends to be achieved and therefore the means to them cannot be clearly specified. The development of skill in handling unprogrammed situations (some prefer the term 'unstructured', but this begs an important question) is vital to those managers who are going to deal effectively with organizational dramas. The focus is on *discovery*.

What are the conditions that seem to foster the process of learning by discovery? There are at least ten that seem to be helpful:

1 Strong commitment to learning on the part of those involved, preferably an interest in the *process* of effective discovery and not only the *product* or outcome.
2 An acceptance by participants that they cannot achieve what they want by a 'programmed' solution.
3 Confidence in one's ability to work effectively at the task.
4 Willingness to accept failures in the attempt to find a solution (from participants and others).
5 External sources of motivation (eg approval from people valued by the participants, promotion, money payments).
6 The participants' existing level of skill in complex problem-solving ('learning to learn').
7 Freedom to work at one's preferred pace, in 'steps' of a size preferred by the participant.
8 Opportunities to work in a situation relevant to the learning-task (as compared with trying out solutions in simulated conditions or in verbal discussion).
9 Continuing feedback on progress in the situation.
10 Availability of help in working at the task: (a) in clarifying issues by acting as 'sounding boards', (b) in maintaining morale.

Rather than discuss each of these, though they are complex enough to make this a useful exercise, we shall discuss three themes into which these conditions can be roughly grouped: (i) motivation, whether from the intrinsic satisfaction of the learning-task or from extrinsic rewards, (ii) skill in setting up and working on a learning task of some complexity, whether this is provided by the learner or by those who are helping him, and (iii) external supports from the situation, such as available time, feedback and opportunity to experiment.

Motivation

It is not surprising that half of the conditions that we have listed are concerned with motivation. The major difficulty with 'discovery learning' is the tremendous frustration that the learner encounters in tolerating failures, slow progress and the occasional tantalizing breakthrough which then proves misleading in its implications. Perhaps because a good deal of education and training has been highly programmed, and incompetence has been strongly criticized by over-eager and well meaning teachers, participants in 'discovery learning' often find that they are constantly regretting wasted time and are inclined to engage in a kind of 'magical thinking' that regards every problem as having a unique solution. Because of these motivational difficulties, it has often been suggested that high external rewards are singularly inappropriate in 'discovery learning', partly because such learning is difficult to reward equitably, and partly because of fears that high rewards might induce a disastrous 'short-circuiting', in which the manager's eagerness to obtain the reward would lead to ineffective solutions of a quasi-routine kind. In our view, the matter warrants further investigation in specific contexts. Motivation is the factor most often ignored in the organization of work, even at the managerial level where it is of vital importance, and the 'pay-off' from systematic study of the best combination and timing of the conditions favouring discovery learning is likely to be enormous.

Skill

It is commonplace to stress the importance of intelligence in selecting managers for work involving discovery learning. The assumption is often made that such work is more appropriate for graduates than others. Probably there is some overlap between 'intelligence' in the sense used in 'intelligence testing' and the skills needed in discovery learning, but the issue needs further clarification. Discovery learning requires skills in thinking around a problem in a flexible rather than a fixed way, the ability to take advantage of hunch and intuition without sacrificing critical awareness. These qualities are more akin to creativity and imagination than formal intelligence. The recent work on 'lateral thinking',[1] 'divergent thinking', and 'the helicopter mind'[2] suggests that the intellectual skills of management are complex and not to be reduced simply to ability to store information quickly and accurately or to work efficiently on well-defined problems (which are the skills assessed in the 'run of the mill' intelligence tests used in educational and vocational selection).

The use of auxiliary skills, whether we call the suppliers of such skills tutors, consultants, catalysts or trainers (eg in sensitivity training), has not been well developed by the educational system. Consultants have often developed these skills from practical experience of working with senior management in handling their complex, stressful situations.

Situational factors

The strongest motivation and the most effectively developed skills can be negated if the situation is irrelevant or fails to provide feedback. It is true that the whole concept of a 'situation' leads us into formidable problems of definition, but we have in mind the rather obvious

[1] Edward de Bono *Lateral Thinking for Management: a handbook of creativity*, McGraw Hill, 1971.

[2] H Muller *The Search for the Qualities Essential to Advancement in a Large Industrial Group: an exploratory study*, 1970 Carel van Bylandtlaan 30, The Hague.

57

matters of enabling people engaged in 'discovery learning' to apply their learning in relevant working situations, with the opportunity of knowing how well or badly they are doing. This has been a serious weakness in many programmes, leading into a labyrinth of simulation and game-like activities which have sometimes weakened rather than strengthened the manager's ability to make a considered judgement of his own effectiveness.

The relevant conditions of discovery learning can best be provided through the medium of development projects, which relate to the dramas of organizational life (and especially development dramas though breakdown dramas can provide, as we have seen, admirable development opportunities for the manager). The concept of a development project requires careful definition and analysis because there are many different kinds of project; we have no wish to criticize existing development programmes for adding to managerial confusion, and then to fall headlong into the same trap.

Development projects

It seems worth distinguishing between three kinds of projects from the point of view of management development. First, there is the kind about which we have been rather lukewarm—the *education or training project*. This is controlled (by virtue of being designed and evaluated) by the training staff to bring about results deemed desirable for training purposes. Business games, group planning, team development exercises and the familiar case discussions are all examples of educational projects. The common element lies in participation of the group in working out a best approach to a given situation (this may be an opportunity but is more often a problem—which itself says something about the flavour of such projects).

The second type is the *management development project*. It is focussed on whatever experiences are likely to develop the professional effectiveness of a manager or group of managers. The location of the project is of vital importance. The education project usually runs in an education and training centre, because skilled staff are scarce and the work takes place around them (and their increasingly elaborate and expensive hardware, which is likely to increase their immobility). Development projects are much more likely to be placed in the context of a job.

The Inter-University Programme for Advanced Management, which runs in Belgium, is an example of a development project. It is mainly the result of the efforts of a British management educator, Professor R W Revans. In this programme, individual senior managers spend some months in organizations which are not their own, working on central problems which do not call for any of the manager's specialist skills. Participants are supported by university staff supervisors and have a number of more 'structured' activities to prepare them for the development project part of the programme. Another example of a programme based on development work is that now being offered by our own institution, the Manchester Business School. Teams of managers work on a problem or opportunity within their own organization in association with members of our faculty who are concerned with making possible the management development pay off from this activity. Following successful trials, this form of development project is now taking its place as one of the major programmes offered by the Business School, under the name of Joint Development Activity (JDA). It is more conservative in scale than the Belgian design: it consists of three month's work part-time (spread over a year) rather than a year full-time; working within one's own rather than in an outside organization; and working as part of a team of managers from the same organization rather than as part of a mixed group, each with an individual task.

The third type of project is the *organizational development (or change) project*. This is a 'project' in a much wider sense, a real change for the better through some clear and significant action: the establishment of a new operating unit, a move to a new location, the acquisition of another company, the setting up of a new production line, the introduction of a computer. All are occasions for organizational projects and, not surprisingly, since they are concerned with the future effectiveness of the organization, the selection of management to take part is given considerable attention by top management.

The three kinds of development projects are all concerned with *participation* on the part of the managers involved, but the guidance offered to the participating manager varies enormously between the three. Referring back briefly to the metaphors of management and management development, one could argue that all the projects are medical or military: their emphasis on active learning distinguishes them from the approaches based on the building and engineering metaphors.

If we think of development as a remedial activity, in which people correct their weaknesses (as in the medical metaphor), the gap between the first and third of these types of project is vast. Organizational projects are given the best available talent. But all would agree that taking part is a wonderful development experience for even the most able and experienced manager. This is a clear example of the contrast between *incidentally* providing a resourceful man with an opportunity to achieve real personal developmental work, and *focussing on* a 'vehicle' for correcting the weaknesses of a manager, as judged by some criterion of overall effectiveness.

We are now concerned here with ways of developing managers systematically rather than incidentally. This calls for careful planning, because our model suggests that projects in this middle ground have a large element of ritual. We shall therefore devote the rest of this survey to looking at ways in which we can rescue the management development project from the fate of being seen as ritual in the pejorative sense. For a grim fate it would be. Management development must be set free, under conditions that encourage success rather than contained in a ritual dance, by development projects. We have already mentioned the tendency for dramas, on repetition, to run down into a routine through sheer familiarity, unless there are special conditions of relevance to key values which delay the process. So projects, unless each is carefully considered in the situation in which it is likely to occur, can easily become habitual routines. This becomes inevitable if one starts with familiar problems (a commonly encountered way of 'playing safe', which contains the development activity within well recognized boundaries). We are not denying the importance of ritual: indeed, its management is important for managers. Its total lack in the technocrat may be one of the technocratic manager's most serious defects, foreshadowed and to some extent corrected in Britain by the establishment of the Administrative Staff College at Henley, briefly described in the samples of management development in the second chapter.

Education for the management of ritual is one thing: the swaddling of management development in the trappings of ritual is quite another; it is to this, and to nothing else, that we object.

The possibilities of keeping management development projects lively and realistic are roughly three-fold. First, the projects can be linked with organizational projects, but not so closely as to lose the possibility of achieving some awareness of personal learning and needs for clearer understanding.

Secondly, the projects can be set up by the participants within the realm of their own experience and interest. They will then spontaneously choose themes which are, *from their point of view*, a blend of the controllable and the realistic. Most managers, and particularly those with operating experience, will reason that they can easily get lost if they do not keep some measure of control, but the whole project will be meaningless if they are not widely seen as having an organizational pay off.

Thirdly, the project can grow out of a formal course but can gradually take on added realism and responsibility as the manager (or group of managers) begins to relate what he has learned on the course to the realities of organizational life. The application of what he has learned then becomes an activity in its own right, rather than an extension of what he has learned to his existing job.

In this last example, the distinction between application within a project and application within one's job may seem strained. Perhaps this is so where managers have great discretion in their jobs (such as managers in research activity). But managers in well established operating jobs may find it difficult to apply what they have learned within their jobs, unless they have learned specific techniques for improving existing operations. The advantage of a development project is that it is sensitive to the application of learning *by its nature*. This suggests that management development projects are particularly at home in 'development management'.

Development projects and development management

The most obvious place for development projects is thus in the parts of the organization concerned with development. The operational forms of management certainly provide many opportunities for a manager to develop his skills, but these are within a fairly clear-cut pattern of requirements. It is only in the development management areas, such as marketing, research and development, development finance and organization development, that it is possible for two opportunities to be grasped together: the development of managers and development of the organization.

Many organizations have recognized this in their use of 'bright young graduates', especially the expensive graduates in business administration. They have put them into a function such as marketing and computers or even in an ill-defined area called corporate strategy. But there has been an unhappy diffusion and dispersion of these efforts because the development activities of the firm have not been sufficiently co-ordinated. As a result, the graduates are not only likely to be isolated and even overwhelmed within their scattered development activities: the very opposite can happen and they can be sucked into the welter of operational routines or operational breakdown.

Bringing about change, in managers and in the organization itself, through the use of projects has the advantage of making it possible to see how far managers can be led into the major organizational change projects through controlled management development projects. At present, such changes are often not thought of in these terms and as a result the development of individuals and of the organization can get seriously out of phase. Some organizational change may be achieved at the expense of the effective career development of some of the individuals taking part in it, since it may cause them to be grossly overloaded or seriously diverted from their preferred career paths. Also, the career aspirations of individuals may be pursued at the expense of the best interests of the organization (this is often, unfortunately, called 'organizational politics' thus contaminating a useful phrase and preventing its use in a more neutral form).

Although the major argument in these notes is that management development and development management can offer a good deal to one another, it must not be thought that we entirely ignore the management development potential of operations management. General management too is not only an understandable goal of the more ambitious forms of management development but could in a sense be said to constitute its major operational test.

There are three points to make on the issue of relating development projects to operational management: first, the importance of helping development management to contribute effectively to operations management, rather than becoming detached and fragmented, on the one hand, or swallowed up entirely in operations on the other. Secondly, a vital contribution can be made to improving the quality of operations management, so that it moves purposefully towards well established objectives and makes the best use of available operating routines and techniques. Small improvements are of enormous importance in large scale operations, and it must always be remembered that improvements in production costs of the order of one per cent can bring savings in five figures in large operating systems, as in steel, gas, electricity and petrochemicals. Management training and education are the answers: better development management through management development can lead to the setting of more effective objectives for these activities.

Thirdly, trouble-shooting or breakdown management: operations, however well protected, can always break down. Sometimes the breakdowns, once they have occurred, can be readily traced and corrected and these can be assimilated to the routine operations. But more serious breakdowns may take great skill to understand and resolve. Trouble shooting of this kind is a high-ranking activity in all operating units, as we have seen, and is often a 'fast track' to the top.

Some differences between development management and operations management

One usually thinks of development managers as fairly radical, especially those in marketing or the research part of research and development. Trouble-shooters, in our experience, are anything but radical. They are somewhat disenchanted people, hardened by their experience of suffering, human inadequacy and the 'seamy side' of organizational life (and death). If this sounds like a stereotype, drawn directly from television plays, we would reply that people and events often take on the form of a stereotype and 'trouble-shooting' more than most.

Nevertheless, all is not sweetness and light in the development world. Developments often suffer setbacks, and the tendency in many organizations to control developments very closely with budgets and elaborate planning schedules can bring them into almost the same difficulties as the operations sector when failures occur. A strong argument for keeping the development sector distinguished from the sphere of operations is that a confusion between the two invariably leads to inadequate development. For example, the development resources are subjected to operational criteria of effectiveness, which leads to their being seen as wasteful and self-indulgent (Clerk Maxwell's "What use is a baby?" is the classic defence against such reasoning, but a defence that has continually to be made whenever development is not judged by appropriate criteria). Another common tendency is for development people to be drawn into trouble-shooting. Two reasons are given for this: development people can be spared while operations people cannot; and trouble-shooting requires the exercise of resourcefulness and ingenuity, just like development.

Many of the more insecure development people will accept a trouble-shooting role, on the ground that this will enable them to achieve 'credibility' by establishing their competence. Alas, if they succeed, they have firmly established their competence—as trouble-shooters and, in any complex organization in a changing environment there is always trouble to be shot.

Putting the distinction between trouble-shooting and development rather fancifully, and using the 'steady state' as the central theme of operations, we could see the mainstream operations manager as a 'solid' man, the development manager (if protected from attrition) as a 'light' man and the trouble-shooter as a 'leathery' man. Each of these qualities can be viewed positively or negatively (they are rarely seen neutrally, and we have deliberately chosen colloquial rather than objective labels to reflect this characteristic). Positively viewed, the solid man is reliable, predictable, trustworthy, stable, reasonable, sensible, mature; the light man is lucid, brilliant, imaginative, far-seeing, creative, spirited; and the leathery man is resourceful (the very pattern of the hero implied in the military metaphor of management), courageous, dynamic, adaptable, invulnerable, commanding. Negatively viewed, the solid man becomes pedestrian, dull, mediocre, conformist, reactionary; the light man becomes untrustworthy, obscure, vapid, insubstantial, cosmic, expendable; and the leathery man becomes unfeeling, autocratic, abrasive, aggressive, and self-seeking.

The general manager is, in the popular view of writings on general management, an all-rounder—a powerful and stable mixture of lightness, solidity and leatheriness. If this cannot be achieved (and the mixture sounds both unusual and possibly unstable), then the all-roundness must be expressed adequately in the top management group. Our impression of senior British management is that solidity, leatheriness and lightness are expressed in roughly the ratio 6:3:1. Perhaps this is somewhat overstating the proportion of lightness!

In conclusion

The argument in this chapter has moved from a discussion of the main types of managerial activity, and their development in different programmes of learning and teaching, to the groupings of these activities into operations management, development management and general management. We focussed on the need in British management to give high priority to the strengthening of 'development management'. Three kinds of development projects were briefly discussed.

5 The future of management development

In a sense, the whole of the preceding discussion has been about the future of management development, because it has focussed on trends that are only just becoming apparent in the mainstream of British management thinking and practice.

At this point we want to look at some of the conditions that seem particularly relevant to fostering effective forms of development. Three that merit further discussion are (1) the role of the British business schools and related centres of management development (2) the need for a new kind of 'management teacher', and (3) some relevant aspects of what is currently called organization development.

The future of the British Business schools

The activities of the major schools can be roughly divided into three parts: teaching, research and consultancy. Teaching covers an enormous variety of programmes and methods, but is always concerned with helping individuals to learn. This is usually done in 'courses' of one kind or another, in educational or training centres away from the immediate workplace. Research is given particular emphasis by the university schools (though independent centres, such as Ashridge and Henley, are also putting more weight on it). Most of the research takes the form of relatively long-term investigations into problem areas of management and business (typical projects last three to five years), conducted by individuals or teams who expect to publish their results. The conflict between 'rigour' and 'relevance' in many fields of research is well known and is still unresolved in the business schools. Managers want to know what to do in highly individual and changing situations. Research findings deal in tendencies and generalities. They look for patterns occurring under stated conditions. Some of these findings, out of context, seem banal and unhelpful to the experienced manager. Nevertheless, many issues can be studied systematically and evidence can be collected, organized and made available to those interested to study and test for themselves.

The third activity of the schools is regarded with some suspicion both in business, in management and in the academic world. Consultancy is often confidential, particular and profitable, while research is public, general and costly. In the major schools, staff are allowed (and even encouraged within limits) to practise consultancy, as long as it contributes to the competence of the consultant and is not merely hackwork bringing in additional income. Some of this consultancy is highly regarded by the organizations for which it is provided, and has undoubtedly contributed to establishing the reputation of certain senior members of business school faculties and, by extension, the schools themselves.

The most valuable trend for the future would be (and to some extent is) a convergence of these three activities. Consultancy is perhaps the most idiosyncratic and flexible of the three, since it grows out of a perceived need and is based on mutual trust between members of the organization and the consultancy service. Consultancy can lead to both research and teaching. One could argue that the exploratory forms of consultancy (and these are the most appropriate for the schools) can be readily seen as 'action-research' or as a form of teaching.

Universities usually encourage their staff to learn lecturing by a kind of osmosis. To a lesser extent, the able students who get good degrees and become members of university staffs also learn to run discussion groups, prepare and deliver research papers at seminars and take part in tutorials. But in most universities, these skills are not learned with the same thoroughness as lecturing (if one accepts, as we do, that constant listening contributes, largely unconsciously, to sets of expectations and skills).

With its tradition of rather formal speaking for 50 minutes followed, if at all, with answers to a few questions, lecturing does not fit in well with the give-and-take of a consulting relationship. But the more informal methods of teaching have a much stronger kinship.

In much the same way, the extended and formal (we nearly said ritualistic) types of academic research have little in common with consultancy, even when a consulting relationship is expressed at some stage in a formal report. Such reports follow a logic of their own, which seldom match the logic of a research report, except in the special case of consultancy reports that are pieces of externally provided research (for example, in a technical field or possibly in marketing). But the shorter, crisper approach of action-research, with working papers, exchange of memoranda, transcriptions of conference between practitioners, has a great deal in common with consultancy.

The university schools must remember that they have a duty to the universities as well as to business and management. They must make formal contributions to theory and not only informal contributions to current practice. They must experiment and report and not only manipulate and act. They are practitioners of ideas as well as facts, operators in the future and not only the present.

Let us suppose that the convergence takes place and the delicate balance of the schools is nonetheless preserved. What will be the implications for management development? First, and most obvious, management development in the schools will be a matter of high concern, because they will be concerned with observable improvements in the effectiveness of managers and not only the individual learning of people attending their courses. The whole concept of a 'course' will be replaced by 'ways of improving effectiveness'.

Secondly, and following from the increase of interest within the schools, development will be seen as a complex series of processes about which all too little is known. Instead of focussing on the materials that managers should learn, at the expense of the ways in which the materials can be learned, the processes of learning will be given at least as much attention as what managers need to know and do.

Thirdly, this means that the relationship between development and learning will be given attention. If we define development as an increase in scale, complexity and integration (individually or in combination), it is clear that some integration happens without learning; for example, by a genetically controlled process of maturing. And some learning, far from being developmental, may be destructive, like learning to weaken one's self and others.

It seems clear that these changes will have profound implications for those highly organized forms of learning that have evolved as the universities' contribution to professional training (the degree and diploma courses, lasting one year to five or six years full-time). In the business and management worlds, the MBA and related postgraduate qualifications will have to face, and find an answer to, the question "What relevance do you have to the development of managerial competence?" It will not escape the reader that this question is already being asked, but the answers go little beyond assertions that professions always have long, formal programmes of higher education (but, alas, these too are facing interrogation, which is all the more harsh when the questions are resented, and the answers are either evasive, ignorant or assertive).

The award of degrees and diplomas raises the difficult question, too, of the status of management as a profession. It seems to be more of an art than a science, more of a satisfying and complicated job (or set of jobs which can be tackled in every conceivable order) rather than a profession in the usual orderly sense. Be this as it may, the business of management development, profession or not, will have to be achieved in many more places than the centres of development 'programmes'. The university schools will be in the strongest position to run the more extended, research-based programmes. Until now this has suggested that they are mainly concerned with the young manager, at the outset of his career, before he has become too valuable to spare from his job. This may well continue to be true but the arrival of newer forms of management organization, which place less operating weight on the top echelons, may enable senior people to work in or with schools for extended periods, on a part-time assignment, on secondment as members of research programmes or teaching-programmes.

The need for a new kind of 'management teacher'

We have been at some pains to avoid the suggestion that 'management development' is merely a glorified name for management education and training courses. We have also tried to indicate the inadequacies of expecting management development to emerge smoothly and effectively in the course of a typical management career, especially the typical 'operational careers'. We see development as occurring in jobs including specially devised jobs in development groups and in learning programmes. These learning programmes require new kinds of expertise in the staff who take part in designing, participating (as consultants, specialists, experts etc) and in evaluating them.

We must try to avoid the temptation to conjure a 'man for all seasons' out of the requirements. We are no more likely to find him (except occasionally) than we are to find the all-round managing director or the complete marketing man. But we can nevertheless begin to state the requirements for staff members of a management development centre and to estimate the likely types of people who would, between them, meet these requirements.

Facing a similar task, the members of a NEDO panel on management teachers described four kinds of teachers in the present management *education* system: the academic, the techniques man, the ex-business manager and the business graduate. They are defined by their experience and training and are seen as having characteristic strengths and weaknesses. For example, quoting from the first report of the panel (NEDO 1970) for the academic, "His powers of analysis and abstraction have to be set against a lack of an inter-disciplinary conceptual approach. His training in model-building in a single discipline may confine his studies to unreal problems which provide no illumination of real and complex business situations". Or the practising manager, (his) "empiricism and pragmatism need to be distilled, dissected and categorized in order to be put to work in management education. This he often cannot do". With the techniques man, there is usually "good practical experience", but "the key problem is the need for breadth of outlook". There is a warning that techniques and the context in which they are applied change rapidly "so that the techniques teacher may, unless he is keeping in close touch with developments in this subject area and with industry, be sharpening obsolete weapons". And the postgraduate, even, "finds himself faced with teaching a multiplicity of objectives in which priority and purpose are ill-defined. He often takes refuge in advancing one area of study . . . He may also fail to pay sufficient attention to developing himself as a member of a teaching team . . ." These comments, based on experience of working in management education centres, are perceptive and useful in looking for gaps in management education (though one of the present authors, John Morris, must plead to bias, as a member of the panel writing the report), but we have still not succeeded in finding an elegant and economical typology of teachers.

There are other ways of tackling the problem of requirements. Following our analysis, we suggest that they fall into at least four groups. First, the basic distinction between operations, development and general management. Secondly, the basic functional distinction between major parts of the operational task: inputs, transformations and outputs (roughly corresponding to gaining resources from appropriate markets in the environment of the organization, converting them into the selected goods/services and making them available to appropriate markets). This 'open system' approach is becoming more and more popular in management development centres. But there has been little attempt so far to organize the work of the centre— in research, teaching and consultancy—around these activities and their inter-relations. Third comes the distinction between three broad 'subject clusters'—economic/financial, behavioural and quantitative. These have developed by stages from the academic disciplines of economics, mathematics, statistics, sociology and psychology. Our view is that this particular grouping should really be seen as a simple matrix: the two-fold distinction between economic/financial materials and behavioural materials on the one hand and the distinction between quantitative and non-quantitative approaches to handling information on the other. Because business schools have linked the quantitative approach with the economic/financial area more closely than with the behavioural area (for fairly obvious reasons), the belief has grown that behavioural matters are of great importance but by their very nature cannot be quantified, while the economic/financial area is an 'exact science'. This has had unfortunate effects on credibility as the conventional and ritual underpinnings of accounting practice are revealed, and the importance of getting measures of 'business confidence' (a behavioural variable) becomes increasingly evident. But we are now briskly riding a hobby-horse.

The functional specialism of manufacturing organizations, such as purchasing, production, sales and distribution and marketing are likely to continue as a fourth grouping of management development centre requirements, even though they seem unduly 'practical' to some staff members of centres. The reason for this is simply that these functional divisions represent a convenient adaptation of the structure of the development centre to the structure of the organizations with which they are working.

These four groupings bring out clearly the formidable problems of conceptual integration within the centres. From the educational world, staff members have acquired qualifications in economics, commerce, mathematics, statistics, psychology, sociology or government. Only in business schools have there been 'integrative' or applied areas such as managerial economics, business psychology, industrial sociology, or even 'analysis of the business environment' or 'business policy'.

Our problem comes, as we suggested at the outset, from using a framework for looking at management development that is not yet established as either a clearly recognizable operational reality or a development system (though much of what we have been discussing is already in being, such as the development segments of the operating functions).

It may sound facile to say that helping to clear up this conceptual confusion will be one of the most important tasks of the new-style management centre staff. Nevertheless this is a proposal that we feel bound to make. As long as the main offerings of formal development programmes consist of fragmented courses, with material on marketing, sales, computers, information systems, staff development, personnel management, economic environment and quantitative methods, the confusion will continue.

We would certainly be over-facile if we ended the discussion here. We can extract from the points made so far the following guides to actions:

1 Staff members will need to recognize the value of using the specialist experience of participating managers as a constructive and vital part of the programmes of the centres.

2 They will need constantly to look for integrative links within their development programmes, using a general-systems approach as the broad framework.

3 From this approach the most central themes are (i) the maintenance and development of the organization as a viable system (to use Beer's useful term), (ii) the

contribution of the environment to organizational possibilities and (iii) the contribution of the organization to its members and to the environment.

Where will the new-style staff members get their training? Without wishing to quibble, we suggest that they will not have been *trained* but will have *developed* themselves, with appropriate facilities. That is, they will not have 'done' well defined courses, ending with a set of formal qualifications 'licensing' them as qualified teachers, researchers or consultants. They will have developed understanding rather than knowledge, abilities rather than technical skills, personal values rather than currently fashionable 'attitudes'.

Organizational development in theory and practice

The rather grandiose term 'organizational development' has been variously defined. The most ambitious form is 'a planned change in the activities of the total organization'. This is tantamount to a take-over bid for the policy-making and corporate strategy functions. A more modest definition is 'the systematic development of the people constituting an organization to engage in change whenever it is appropriate'. Here the focus of attention is the people: the individuals, working groups, and the relationships between them. The 'organization', in this sense, is the social system—the human organization—rather than the totality of resources engaged on the productive and distributive processes. Confusion often results from such varied uses of 'organization'.

When one considers the actual instances of activities going on under the rubric of 'organizational development', one finds that they neither engage in corporate strategy nor are they concerned with the organization in its wider human aspects. Instead, one finds groups of people attending short intensive courses, focusing on individual attitudes and the on-going forms of group behaviour. The most frequently encountered forms of 'organizational development' in this sense are the 'managerial grid' of Blake and

Mouton[1]. Coverdale training, human relations group training and 'sensitivity training' (the sensitivity being an awareness of individuals and group needs).

Defenders of such activities point out that the training in question is merely a systematic preparation for later work within the organization itself. The task of this training is to equip the course participants with a common language and an awareness of the great improvements that can follow from individual and group commitment to planned change throughout the organization. A study of the literature of organizational development reveals a careful distinction between phases of development, ranging from seven to nine, each of which takes the concepts, skills and underlying motivational supports a step further towards the complete co-ordination of all the activities into what Blake and Mouton have called the pursuit of corporate excellence.

Unfortunately, the programmes rarely show any progression beyond the first stage or two; and studies of the translation of concepts and methods into the day to day activities of the organization usually show some encouraging but rather slight changes in commitment, plus the development of skills in running meetings, but little that is really impressive.

Why is this? We can only offer conjecture. Perhaps it is simply that the rituals and routines are so well established in human organization that attempts to change them rarely get beyond the early stage. The dramas initiated by the intensive training programmes are rapidly dampened by the mass of routines and even the most enthusiastic supporter loses heart. Another possibility is that (to use the language of gamesmanship) 'organizational development' is a bid by management development and personnel specialists to gain influence over the policy-making and planning activities of the organization. Such

[1] BLAKE R R and MOUTON J S. *Corporate excellence through grid organizational development.* Gulf Publishing Company, Houston, Texas, 1968.

a bid for leadership can usually be readily countered by the other 'development functions'—research and development, marketing, development finance and operational research. If there is any truth in this conjecture, two things can be said. First, given the actual status and influence of most management development and personnel specialists, such a take-over bid seems an unrealistic strategy. Secondly, even if the strategy were to be successful, it would still be mistaken, in our view, because a single functional specialism, however important, cannot adequately represent the whole range of organizational concerns (using the term 'organization' now in its wider sense).

In their role as students of organization, management development specialists are clearly aware of the dangers of the specialized part speaking for the whole (unless it is the general management function): it is therefore ironic that they should fall into the trap of feeling that they have a special claim to the universal viewpoint.

The difficulties of organization development in finding a viable role *as a distinguishable activity* draw attention to the continuing identity problems of personnel management. Every form of organizational specialization turns out on inspection to present formidable problems of definition and setting of boundaries. Even the mainstream activities of production, sales and finance find their relations to one another changing bewilderingly. But no other specialized function is so closely identified with the most volatile, self-conscious organizational resource—the only resource that is a source of value in its own right.

No wonder that personnel managers oscillate between extremes that range from doubts as to the need for their existence to dreams of setting the corporate strategy. One can meet personnel managers who are more technocratic, objective and hard-nosed than the general managers whom they are zealously serving. There are personnel managers who feel they have a duty to represent and serve the personal values that their organizations, through top management decisions, are flouting at every turn. This is not surprising: personnel management is the function through which organizations reveal their attitudes and values to the people who constitute them and these are often confused and conflicting.

There is a clear need, then, for personnel managers to recognize that they are not just doing a straightforward no-nonsense job, but are a point of intersection of some of the most important human issues of organization. The phrase 'point of intersection' is itself too cool. 'Arena' would not be too strong a term, though many personnel managers would prefer 'forum'. The organizational dramas of development and breakdown cannot be segregated into training centres, though it is clear that some innocuously-labelled 'training programmes' are really powerful adventures in personal development that make the day to day routines of some jobs appear grey and inhuman. If personnel managers toy, as they are often tempted to, with the role of *éminence grise* they must remember that it is among the most dangerous and corruptible of roles. In our view, a major value of linking personnel activities with development management is that relevance and clarity of purpose are combined. The diverse development functions provide an excellent opportunity to make personnel management dramatic without losing reality. There is also encouragement for the activities of personnel management to be openly rather than covertly political. The personnel manager finds that he himself has embarked on a project of self-discovery.

In place of a conclusion

Robert Graves has written a poem which ends half-way through a line, taking off in mid-career in a manner that is both admirable and poetic. As we have argued, management development can easily become prosaic—the management career becomes a beaten track and dramas run down into mere routines.

We have therefore resisted the temptation to condense our notes into a well-rounded conclusion. They are already over-assertive, leaving many connections unexplored, open-ended to a fault. But some of our themes may bear re-stating briefly.

Initially we looked at how managers see management development, and at some case studies of management development activities at the organizational level. In these we detected an area of management development which we judge to have been relatively neglected in formal and specialist writing and prescriptions for management development. It was the sort of development that has its impact on a man's ability to succeed in the messy, uncertain, dynamic and highly critical areas of management activity; in a word, the development of resourcefulness.

We attempted in chapter 3 to present our 'model', in terms of drama, ritual and routine. We believe this model has some value because it admits to management development the organic aspect of management development which we found in the metaphors and case studies, and at the same time relates this to the better understood aspects of education and training.

A major theme in the remaining chapters has been to trace through some of the implications of this elusive and organic aspect of management development. In particular we related it on the one hand to aspects of organizational functioning and on the other to the processes of learning involved, and through this to strategies of management development.

At the level of organizations we found that 'training' could be regarded as preparation for the programmed activities which abound in the operations function of an organization. 'Development' is preparation for the unprogrammed activities to be found in the development function of organizations (the part that adapts existing operations) and in the operations sector following a serious breakdown. We noted also that, just as development in our sense tends to have been neglected in management development, the development function has been neglected in organization design.

When considering aspects of human learning, we found that organic development is a process of discovery learning. This has many implications for strategies of management development. In general we concluded that development projects in which the participants carry out self-initiated activity in a real (not merely simulated) situation is the only way in which this sort of development can occur.

Managers are deeply concerned with their own development. While they have no wish to be forced to re-discover the wheel, they realize that many of the most important aspects of management effectiveness must be discovered by each manager at first-hand. The task of those who are professionally concerned with management development is important and delicate. It is to find ways of helping managers to develop through managerial work. Managerial work is calling increasingly for the varied qualities of resourcefulness. Management development, then, must never lose contact with those forms of work in which the manager can experiment and become visible to himself and others.

Finally, since we see a need for growth in management development, and are anxious to see it occur, we have three simple statements which we hope set the scene for the future:

1 The development of resourceful managers for handling development and breakdowns is a vital need in Britain.

2 Management development in its wider and more diffuse sense can be usefully divided into training, education and development. All three forms are relevant to organizational needs but it is development that is relevant to the need for resourceful managers, and it is development that is relatively neglected at the moment. Development projects, combining individual career advantage and organizational interests, can play a valuable part in enabling managers to develop themselves.

3 Business schools, management 'teaching', 'organizational development' programmes and sundry other matters of current concern in management development, themselves need a vigorous development activity because they so rapidly become established forms: dramas which run down all too swiftly into rituals and routines.

Appendix : further reading

We have not attempted to summarize the existing literature on management development and related topics in this publication. However, we are indebted to many thinkers, researchers, practitioners and writers whose ideas we have freely adapted to our own use. The list of such influences is too long for us to remember, let alone record and acknowledge individually, but we should like to mention a few studies of particular relevance.

BEER Stafford, *Brain of the Firm, the managerial cybernetics of organization*, Allan Lane, Penguin, 1972, has been a pervasive influence on our thinking generally, and specifically in the distinction made between operations and development management. We judge it to be a real breakthrough in organizational theory, analysing as it does the necessary systemic features of the viable organization.

BENNIS W G, *Organization Development*, Addison-Wesley, Massachusetts, 1969, briefly and simply introduces some of the leading ideas in organization development. The best short introduction to the subject.

COHEN J, *Homo Psychologicus*, Allen and Unwin, 1971. A revision of the author's earlier pioneering work *Humanistic Psychology*. The first chapter contains a brilliant survey of the use of metaphors in psychological theory.

GLICKMAN A S, HAHN C P, FLEISHMAN E A, BAXTER B, *Top Management Development and Succession*, Macmillan, 1968, looks at top managers and their paths to the top; it is that rare achievement: an empirical study that does not get lost in detail.

HUTTON G, *Thinking about Organization*, second edition,

Tavistock Publications, 1972, provides a readable and engaging introduction to organization theory and research. Especially valuable on the Tavistock work.

LAWRENCE P and LORSCH J, *Organization and Environment,* Harvard University Press, 1967, contains a simple and practical analysis of the way in which organizations are differentiated to match the structure of the environments with which they work. The study brings out the vital need for integration in organizational life, and shows the form taken by integration in different types of organization.

LAWRENCE P and LORSCH J, *Developing Organizations: Diagnosis and Action,* Addison-Wesley, Massachusetts, 1969, further develops the implications of the foregoing research.

RAPOPORT Dr R N, *Mid-Career Development: Research Perspectives on a Developmental Community for Senior Administrations,* Tavistock Publications, 1970, was our major source for the description of Henley as an example of a general management development activity. It contains an insight analysis of Henley as a 'developmental community' in striking contrast to business schools, training centres and development projects.

REVANS R W, *Developing Effective Managers. A new approach to business education,* Longman, 1971, is an account of a strikingly original, activity-based management development programme and its rationale. We have little doubt that this book, and the work on which it is based, will become a landmark in the development of managers.

WARR P, BIRD M, RACKHAM N, *Evaluation of Management Training,* Gower Press, 1970, deals with evaluation for planning and control of operations management training, which is the key to the effectiveness of such activities. This is not an activity we have gone into in any depth since it has already had its fair share of attention elsewhere. We commend this book, which is admirably oriented to the needs of the practitioner, to readers concerned with the subject.

Books from IPM

The IPM produces a large number of books on a wide range of management issues. Some of these are described below. For a free catalogue giving details of all our titles (over 95 now) write to the address on the title page. IPM books can be bought from your local bookseller or direct from IPM. Please add 10 per cent to cover postage and packing.

A Textbook of Personnel Management
George Thomason £3.95 (£5.50 hardback)

There have been books on manpower planning, books on training and on industrial relations, but there has long been a desperate need for a book which deals with the complex subject of personnel management as a whole in the British context.

Now at last there is a book to fill that gap – A Textbook of Personnel Management – written by Professor Thomason, Montague Burton Professor of Industrial Relations at University College, Cardiff. The author makes a thorough, detailed assessment of current personnel practice and describes how the function has become what it is. Professor Thomason's expertise in the legislative and industrial relations fields makes this book invaluable to the practising manager as well as to the student.

The Thomason textbook provides ideal background reading and will be indispensable for reference purposes. 536 pages. Second edition, revised throughout.

Recruitment and Selection
P R Plumbley £1.50

Philip Plumbley has revised this best seller, of which *Works Management* wrote: "This is one of the few technical publications which I have been able to read like a novel and I became so engrossed that I found it impossible to put it down until

I reached the final page. It was disappointing to find that it had come to an end."

Staff Appraisal
Randell, Packard, Shaw and Slater £1.30
Since this book was first published the authors have been involved in running some 60 courses covering over 500 managers, and the principles described here are now being used in several large organizations, notably the Delta Metal Company, Beecham Pharmaceuticals and Cheshire County Council. This edition has been brought up to date by incorporating the authors' latest thinking. "... useful to those planning a performance appraisal training programme ... written in a straightforward fashion and brings out some essential points of which any appraisal interviewers should have knowledge."
Personnel Psychology

"A very useful book which would be of tremendous help not only to those who may be responsible for designing and implementing an appraisal scheme but to every manager anxious to improve his skill in staff appraisal."
Industrial Society

A Practical Guide to the Employment Protection Act
Michael Rubenstein £2.00
On its way to becoming law, the Employment Protection Bill underwent many changes. Every manager will need to be fully aware of how the Act's provisions will affect his organization. Michael Rubenstein, a leading journalist in the field of industrial relations here provides expert commentary on the many different provisions of this complex and important new piece of legislation.

The Sex Discrimination Act — a guide for managers
Michael Nash £2.00
This IPM's guide to this vital piece of legislation will enable managers to assess the importance of the Act's provisions to their own organizations.

Developing Effective Managers

Tom Roberts £1.30

Although seven years have passed since the first edition of this book, the need for this kind of publication seems to be as pronounced as ever. The aim is to present, in as readable a form as possible, the main principles on which companies are basing their management development programmes and to discuss some of the more important problems and issues that arise.

This edition tries to incorporate new knowledge, new ideas and new thinking while retaining all that was useful in the principles and practices of seven years ago.

". . . packs into (its) most readable pages far more constructive ideas, lucid analysis and reasoned comment than many weightier volumes."

Technical Education

Personnel Management in Hospitals

Graham Millard £1.30

The book answers a lot of questions on a whole range of personnel management practices in hospital management such as recruitment and selection, training, staff appraisal, records, communications factors affecting morale and making the best use of staff resources. It also aims to promote discussion on practical aspects of personnel management and includes check lists and reference documents, plus some case studies to encourage the reader to relate to reality the range of sound employment practices explained in the book.

Practical Manpower Planning

John Bramham £1.50

This is an easily readable guide for the manager starting in manpower planning or wishing to know more about it.

Contents: 1 The development of manpower planning; 2 The manpower planning process; 3 Identifying manpower requirements; 4 Analyzing manpower supply I; 5 Analyzing manpower supply II – wastage analysis; 6 Formulating manpower planning; 7 Manpower control, reporting and costs; 8 Information for manpower planning;

9 Computers and models in manpower planning; 10 Future developments in manpower planning.

Techniques and Developments in Management — a selection
Margaret Butteriss £1.30
In recent years a bewildering number of developments in management practices have taken place, and every manager needs to be aware of the implications of these changes for his organization. Margaret Butteriss examines new practices which are intended to enable the individual to achieve greater satisfaction from his work, such as job rotation and flexible working hours, as well as techniques and developments which are aimed at achieving corporate needs. Every manager who wishes to keep abreast of current management issues will welcome this IPM paperback.

Basic Personnel Procedures
David Barber £1.00
From time to time personnel managers may find themselves in the position of establishing a personnel department from scratch, setting up basic personnel procedures or perhaps reviewing the organization of work in an existing department. This introductory booklet has been written with these particular problems in mind.

Instant Library?
A set of basic readings on a wide range of management subjects from *Staff Appraisal* to *Recruitment and Selection* in one easy move.
IPM's current catalogue now lists over 95 titles. A complete set of all our publications (everything listed in our new catalogue) is now available for the bargain price of £80 – normal cost over £150.

For details of IPM Courses and Conferences and our Appointments Service (90 per cent of all personnel management vacancies are carried in our journals), or for more details about the Institute itself, write to the address on the title page, or ring 01-387 2844.